Damaged LIVES

PETER LANG
New York • Washington, D.C./Baltimore • Bern
Frankfurt am Main • Berlin • Brussels • Vienna • Oxford

Jeffrey J. Folks

Damaged LIVES

Southern & Caribbean Narrative FROM Faulkner TO Naipaul

PETER LANG
New York • Washington, D.C./Baltimore • Bern
Frankfurt am Main • Berlin • Brussels • Vienna • Oxford

Library of Congress Cataloging-in-Publication Data

Folks, Jeffrey J.
Damaged lives: Southern and Caribbean narrative
from Faulkner to Naipaul / Jeffrey J. Folks.
p. cm.
Includes bibliographical references (p.) and index.
1. American fiction—Southern States—History and criticism.
2. Caribbean fiction (English)—History and criticism. 3. Southern States—
Intellectual life—1865–. 4. Caribbean Area—Intellectual life.
5. Southern States—In literature. 6. Caribbean Area—In literature.
7. Narration (Rhetoric). I. Title.
PS261.F644   810.9'975—dc22   2005006862
ISBN 0-8204-7876-8

Bibliographic information published by **Die Deutsche Bibliothek**.
Die Deutsche Bibliothek lists this publication in the "Deutsche
Nationalbibliografie"; detailed bibliographic data is available
on the Internet at http://dnb.ddb.de/.

Cover design by Sophie Boorsch Appel

The paper in this book meets the guidelines for permanence and durability
of the Committee on Production Guidelines for Book Longevity
of the Council of Library Resources.

© 2005 Peter Lang Publishing, Inc., New York
275 Seventh Avenue, 28th Floor, New York, NY 10001
www.peterlangusa.com

All rights reserved.
Reprint or reproduction, even partially, in all forms such as microfilm,
xerography, microfiche, microcard, and offset strictly prohibited.

Printed in the United States of America

To the memory of my dear parents,
John and Hazel Folks

Contents

	Acknowledgments	ix
	Introduction	1
1.	Faulkner, Canetti, and Survival	11
2.	Ethics Adrift: Faulkner's *If I Forget Thee, Jerusalem*	27
3.	Faulkner's Requiem for the Past	43
4.	Fitzgerald's "Dream of the South"	57
5.	James Agee's Radical Honesty	69
6.	*Wise Blood*: O'Connor's Vision of a Broken World	85
7.	Redemption of Ordinary Delight: Mary Hood's *Familiar Heat*	105
8.	Naipaul's Grief: *The Enigma of Arrival*	119
	Bibliography	131
	Index	135

Acknowledgments

I am grateful to many teachers and colleagues who, over a period of forty years, have nurtured and enlarged my understanding of literature. As a graduate student, I was fortunate to study with Professor James H. Justus, now retired from Indiana University, and later, during a postdoctoral seminar, with Professor Lewis P. Simpson, Boyd Professor Emeritus at Louisiana State University. The late Albert Wertheim, former Dean of Arts and Sciences and Professor of English at Indiana University, during the three decades that I was privileged to know him, served as an exemplar of humane teaching and scholarship. I am also indebted to the many colleagues and students at the institutions where I have taught, not only in America but in Japan and Eastern Europe.

In my study of the relationship of ethics and literature, I continue to learn from the theoretical works of a number of scholars, including Hannah Arendt, Elias Canetti, Leszek Kolakowski, and Alasdair MacIntyre.

Without the loving presence of my wife, Nancy Summers Folks, this book and so much else in life would not have been possible.

I would like to acknowledge permission to reprint the following essay in a revised version: "'Memory Believes Before Knowing Remembers': Faulkner, Canetti, and Survival." Reprinted by permission. *Papers on Language and Literature* 39.3 (Summer 2003). Copyright © 2003 by The Board of Trustees, Southern Illinois University, Edwardsville.

Art is a way of forgiving the world for its evil and chaos.

—Leszek Kolakowski, *The Presence of Myth*

Introduction

In an eloquent obituary for Pope John Paul II, George Weigel wrote of the Pope's understanding that "Western humanism had gone off the rails, collapsing into forms of self-absorption, and then self-doubt, so severe that men and women had begun to wonder whether there was any truth at all to be found in the world, or in themselves" (A14). In his acute diagnosis of the failings of humanism, John Paul II clarified the difficult spiritual condition of Western democracies and the challenge posed by a heedless rejection of the very possibility of religious faith. While the writers studied in this book have pursued different paths in their quest, each has found his or her fiction shaped by a similar sense of absence and disorder, and most have attempted acts of recovery, renewal, or new creation in response to the damaging self-doubt of their times.

A culture of radical skepticism, based on a groundless faith in reason alone and in the millenarian confidence in the perfectability of human nature, emerged in the post-Enlightenment and since that time has increasingly influenced contemporary literature and culture, undermining all inherited forms of tradition and belief. Lacking such bases of belief, the general culture is set adrift without the ground of authority or purposeful action that had forever been embodied in mythic narratives of faith. So widespread has the automatic reflex of skepticism become that it can be maintained, as it has been by philosophers and critics from Paul Ricoeur to Gabriel Josipovici, that we now live within a culture of suspicion. The inclination of the news media to discern an insidious conspiracy beneath the surface of events is matched by the corrosive temper of cultural critics in the humanities who find that all seemingly "normal" aspects of human civilization are tainted by the selfish motives of greed and power. As the culture of suspicion feeds on itself, growing ever more cynical of the possibility of altruism in any form, the capacity to conceive of a purposeful existence becomes ever more difficult.

In the absence of compelling narratives of belief that once lent their support to the conviction in the meaningfulness of life, there exists a widespread confusion as to the purpose and "shape" of existence or, for that matter, as to whether existence has any purpose at all. In place of such grand narratives, contemporary literature, for the most part, offers little more than a thin diet of derisive humor, contemptuous of conventional society and of the efforts of ordinary human beings to make sense of their lives. The smirking, dismissive quality of this writing reflects an underlying rejection of all positive bases of ethical action. Committed to a posture of relativism and contingency, this writing is preoccupied with the negative task of deconstructing the past. The predictable result is a growing sense of self-doubt, and this cultural skepticism leads directly to the evils of self-destructive indifference and contempt.

The inability of philosophical skepticism to explain the world as it is experienced, to say nothing of its inability to change that world, has gradually led writers from widely different backgrounds to question its basis. One could easily compile an impressive list of such writers from Europe, Asia, the Americas, and elsewhere that would include C. S. Lewis, Thomas Mann, Yukio Mishima, Kenzaburo Oe, Rainer Maria Rilke, Gabriel García Márquez, Alexander Solzhenitsyn, Simone Weil, and others. The destructive effects of radical skepticism are universal, and thus any attempt to restrict the reading along geographical lines is obviously arbitrary. The thesis that I develop in the context of the literature of the American South and the Caribbean could be explored within any modern culture, and, indeed, has been in such studies as Tony Judt's *Marxism and the French Left* and *Past Imperfect: French Intellectuals, 1944–1956*, and in numerous studies of other cultures. Still, a study of the response to the culture of suspicion in the literature of the American South and the Caribbean has much to recommend it, since, I would argue, writers from these regions have experienced the damaging effects of modernity from a perspective outside of the cosmopolitan culture of Britain and the American North, and this perspective affords special insight into the destructive impact of radical skepticism.

By focusing on the conception of "damaged lives," this study examines the consequences of the kind of moral confusion that results in characters like Haze Motes in *Wise Blood* or Charlotte Rittenmeyer and Harry Wilbourne in *The Wild Palms* and of the cultural confusion and degradation that Naipaul, from his unique vantage point, perceives not only in the colonial world but perhaps in a more insidious manner within the cosmopolitan cultures of Britain and America. The damage is evidenced not so much by material want as by a psychological and spiritual deprivation that proceeds from radical doubt concerning the value and meaning of life, but these theories all have the practical effect of lifting restrictions on conduct. The consequence of this "liberation" is a self-indulgent culture in which consumption and narcissistic pleasure prevail over the traditional virtues of humility and self-restraint, yet the paradoxical consequence of such a culture, given the fact that ever-increasing desires can never be gratified, is disillusionment and self-contempt.

The effect of philosophical skepticism on the general culture is thus to create a mentality of apathy and indifference. Within a nihilistic culture one finds an increased level of depression and violence, especially among the young, for the young can least defend themselves against the totalizing arguments of the skeptics. Within a postmodern culture that devalues marriage, it is to be expected that the bonds of marital affiliation are weakened, and the destructive effects of this lost faith in marriage are incalculable. Within a society that teaches the young to question all forms of authority, it is understandable that children grow up in conflict with their parents and with society at large, uncertain of their own identity. Again, the destructive impact is enormous, and it ripples throughout society, affecting families, schools, workplaces, and the community as a whole.

As one would expect, the effect of radical doubt in the sphere of education is especially apparent. Symptomatic of the larger cultural problem, an attitude not only of questioning but of suspicion and scorn is directed toward any teacher who believes in the authority of teaching. Early grade teaching and child-rearing are two human activities in which, at least until recently, an unquestioned authority was attached to the adult for the good reason that young children possess little or no knowledge of most aspects of life and so require, in fact, welcome, tutelage by adults. In the past, the teaching of young children, like child-rearing itself, was, of course, often conducted in the home, indeed, conducted by the parent or guardian so that a seamless continuity existed between formal education and other forms of learning. Yet even in these obvious situations, the need for authority has been dismissed by contemporary theorists such as Jean Piaget, as well as by anti-elitist educational theorists in the United States. John Dewey's belief in the need of the school to adapt to the pupil's needs resulted in an endless flexibility of curriculum designed to bring about a "relevant" educational experience and a radical democratization of academic subjects adapted to student "interests."

It is not by any means only within the arena of education, however, that respect for authority has declined. The political authority of Western democracy, and particularly of the United States, has declined as a result of a spreading climate of suspicion of all power and prestige, not only from without (in the Third World, for example) but from within as well. Skepticism toward Western civilization has focused not only on undermining traditional sources of authority, such as the church or the classical tradition of learning, but also on dismissing the possibility of meaning itself. While he is hardly the most extreme example, Gabriel Josipovici is perhaps typical, as we see in his commentary on *Endgame*: "If we will give up our dreams of domination, of understanding, of fulfillment, of progress, our dreams even of the absurdity of life, then we will be able to attend to" the meaning of Beckett's play (250). The difficulty with this mode of reading is that the basis for meaning that Josipovici claims to discover in writers as various as Homer, Dante, Shakespeare, Proust, and Beckett shifts from one provisional ground to another, none of which seems substantial or enduring enough to engage the sort of mythic conviction necessary to support a workable order. Josipovici's conception of Shakespeare's relation to the craft tradition, for example, begs the question of why one would engage in the craft tradition at all, as does his entire conception of action for its own sake, which, in turn, begs the question of why one would engage in action rather than not do so. If engaging in the craft tradition is the ultimate ground of agency in Shakespeare's case, this seems an inadequate explanation of the motivation behind his enormous accomplishment, since what we mean by "engaging in the craft tradition" is largely the idea of technical apprenticeship. If the central motive for the construction and perpetuation of human civilization consists of nothing more than the emulation of others in terms of professional technique, this is hardly a satisfactory explanation of the enormous sacrifices that human beings have made in the service of civilization.

Clearly, a more compelling basis of belief is called for, given the widespread damage of radical doubt within the general culture. One focus of this study is thus what Paul Elie has referred to as "the convergence of literature and religion" in America. In contrast with Europe, the Bible "retained its authority in America, and, perhaps, it was only natural that the religiously charged books of early modernity would prompt certain American writers to seek out actual religious experience and then to set about writing literary work which would have a frankly religious power" (xi–xii). Such a reading is particularly relevant, of course, to the four Catholic writers on whom Elie focuses, but it is relevant as well to a broad spectrum of modern writing from the Americas. In reaction to the earnest but futile search for meaning in the work of modernist and postmodernist authors, certain postwar writers began to seek a more stable ground of authority and belief. While this search would lead in different directions, it was motivated by a common recognition of the damage that had been caused by the wholesale rejection of inherited forms of belief.

Perhaps the most damaging aspect of this narrow-minded rejection is the reflexive manner in which so-called cultural theorists attempt to undermine the idea of the purposeful life in all its forms. It is as if academics compete with one another in devising more and more clever ways of restating a point derived from Nietzsche: that faith as we have known it has lost its basis of conviction, and that only a complete revolution of ideas can lead us toward a future in which we can exist at all, although we will not exist in the "purposeful" manner that we once imagined. Whatever the motive for this destructive skepticism—perhaps it is actually the guilt of a privileged class that finds itself in a world in which few enjoy such privilege—its effect is pernicious, for eventually it leads the broader culture to question its own right to survive. One symptom of the negativity of recent intellectual endeavor is the current taste for parody, and the more extreme the sneer, the more it is celebrated. Thus, an entire canon of recent cultural studies focused on the bizarre, the twisted, the inverted, and the transgressive is held up as a model of sophistication while anything that smacks of normality is attacked.

Rather than rely on ephemeral critical fashions such as deconstruction and cultural studies, one would do well to fall back on a theoretical tradition of lasting value. In the wake of generations of radical skepticism concerning the validity of religious faith, purposeful order, and ideals of trust and community, several theorists, having weighed the consequences of the rejection of all sources of tradition and authority, have sought to reconstruct workable structures of meaning and *telos*. The recent work of Alasdair MacIntyre, including his astute survey of Western ethical tradition in *After Virtue: A Study in Moral Theory* and his profound consideration of the modern legacy of the Enlightenment in *Whose Justice, Which Rationality?*, constitutes a sophisticated effort to do just that. What MacIntyre offers, however, is far more than merely a history of ethics: his work features a powerful critique of relativism, perspectivism, and nihilism, a critique that serves as an invaluable corrective to generations of careless philosophical endorsements of skepticism. The far-ranging concerns of Elias Canetti, a social philosopher, novelist, dramatist, and memoirist, center on the author's response to the most important moral crisis of the twentieth century, the Holocaust. In his great study of crowd behavior, *Crowds and Power*, Canetti has diagnosed the major spiritual illness of modern culture, that of an extreme reliance on free will and power. While he may have underestimated the potential of inherited traditions of belief to restrain these destructive forces, Canetti understood, perhaps more keenly than anyone in his generation, the instinctual origins of violence and fear.

In the philosophy of Hannah Arendt, one encounters further analysis of the political sources of the centralization and intensification of power in modern society, but Arendt also suggests particular solutions. Although she is unconvinced that it is possible to revert to traditional belief systems, Arendt asserts alternatives to the rule of behaviorism that draw heavily on Judaism and classicism, especially the assertion of the role of the public and private realms articulated in *The Human Condition*. In addition, Arendt's classic study, *The Origins of Totalitarianism*, intends to reverse the influence of a revolutionary climate of thought that draws its force from extreme forms of idealist thinking, a product of the Enlightenment dream of human perfectability. Within this camp of political thought, the ends always justify the means, whatever the cost, since the end is portrayed as a compassionate response to human necessity. In response to the rise of the same forces of totalitarian control, Leszek Kolakowski offers a quite different analysis of both the illness and the cure, but in his own way, Kolakowski is responding to the same reductive forces of materialism that troubled his predecessors.

One of the consequences of extreme skepticism that all of these philosophers perceive is the fragmentation of culture into a plethora of private interests and ad hoc, cult-like belief systems. In the *Ethics*, Aristotle pointed out the impossibility of each individual's having to create ethical culture anew, and he analyzed the damaging consequences to human civilization of the attempt to rely on ad hoc cultures in place of stable, long-standing traditions of belief. Aristotle recognized the vital importance of stability in the laws and moral teachings of society because of the disorder that would ensue if each individual were constantly burdened with the impossible task of constructing a personal system of ethics ex nihilo. The value of inherited cultures, especially those that have been passed down over a long period of time, is that we do not have to create out of nothing or negotiate with others to define common practices and laws. Indeed, one argument in favor of the support of traditional cultures is simply that they can afford to be more relevant to contemporary needs than ad hoc systems of order: beginning with an intricate base of laws, rules, and expectations, they can refine these existing structures of order to meet evolving needs. To toss out an entire system and begin with a newly constructed order such as postmodern culture (as it imagines itself to be) would not only be burdensome but impossible, because, in fact, all newly created cultures, while they pretend to evolve out of nothing, have either drawn their system of rationality to some extent from the past or they exert little practical reason at all, as, for example, does a relativist ethics that makes no qualitative distinction between one action and another. In either case, however, the result is an undermining of the force of inherited belief systems. Even a system that pretends to be revolutionary but is not may be quite damaging since it fosters the illusion that one can live in the absence of a stable consensus of belief, and, in doing so, it opens the door to any sort of social experimentation.

The writers on whom I focus in this book all have been influenced in important ways by the philosophical controversies that I have discussed. As fiction writers, of course, they are not directly concerned with debating ethical issues per se, but they are nonetheless much involved with the task of representing the consequences of shifting conceptions of faith. Among major twentieth-century writers, this consists of representing in imaginative terms the ordeal of confusion and doubt that has resulted from the weakening of inherited belief systems. Even within the canon of work by a single author—William Faulkner is the best example but V. S. Naipaul is certainly another—one can trace the conflict taking place within the general culture, an increasing ambivalence toward and scrutiny of the central values of Enlightenment culture: its progressivism, universalism, and rationalism. In Faulkner's case, a young writer who can be seen to share much of the Enlightenment's rebellion against localism and traditionalism matures into a traditionalist who offers the single word "Believe" as the final injunction to his reader in *Requiem for a Nun*, arguably his last major narrative work. In the thornier case of Naipaul, one encounters a writer who compiles a virtual almanac of human damage, much of it apparently the result of a misguided and arrogant faith in rationalism. At the same time, there is doubt, if not concerning the worth of Western democratic culture, at least concerning the efficacy of religious "superstitions." Naipaul presses the reader beyond the myths of Enlightenment thought but offers no cure-all: there is only an insistence on realism, self-discipline, and honesty.

Faulkner and Naipaul, of course, were not the only major writers to look to the South and the Caribbean as an imaginative boundary that helped to define the identity and mission of the cosmopolitan culture. In the fiction of F. Scott Fitzgerald, a writer from outside the South but one with an important ancestral linkage to the region, "southernness" served, by virtue of its cultural difference, to redefine the national, that is, northern, identity. For many of the writers who shared the pages of the *Saturday Evening Post* with Fitzgerald, Florida and the Caribbean represented an exotic, often decadent, appendage to the national culture—a tropical escape into a sensual dreamland that was nonetheless relatively close at hand. Fitzgerald's depiction of the ignorance, the indolence, the oppressive heat and humidity, and, most importantly, the moral unreliability of the South suggests a cultural perspective that positioned everything "tropical" into a single category of decadent recidivism. By reference to this tropical identity, one could more confidently define the imperial mission of the North, even if this mission failed by enduring standards of virtue and justice.

Drawing on many of the popular stereotypes, Fitzgerald mingled images of impoverished aristocracy with those of crude provinciality in a manner that reflected his profound ambivalence toward the region. While nostalgia for the Old South, or at least a dream of the Old South, played an important role in his characterization of southerners, a more critical and realistic perspective ultimately prevailed. Fitzgerald's sense of disillusionment with the southern subject is especially apparent in his treatment of the New South, which seems to embody all the vices of the commercial North but none of its redeeming features. For Fitzgerald, the South represented a failed ideal, and because it embodied the failure of a cherished dream, the South seemed to summon up his particular resentment.

The failed southern and Caribbean lives that Faulkner, Fitzgerald, and other modernists represented so often in their fiction would be reinterpreted as a sort of "fortunate fall" by Flannery O'Connor, as in her writing regional disadvantage was transmuted into spiritual advantage, an opportunity for grace denied more developed regions. As O'Connor makes clear in her essays, reviews, and letters, one of the implications of her fiction is the *superiority* of a culture that is less progressive in its values, less developed economically, and less educated in regard to secular learning. In O'Connor's mind, by retaining its connections with moral and religious traditions that were being challenged and discarded elsewhere, the South could be understood to be more tolerant, at least more tolerant of faith, than other regions of America. The South's lack of industrialization, of secular education, and of hedonistic indulgence might actually be viewed as a rare cultural opportunity. Conversely, the smug assurance of the secular humanist, as she dramatized in story after story, represented for O'Connor the worst sort of damage.

Similarly, in Mary Hood's fiction, a muted version of the same drama, a less-pointed fortunate fall, is enacted. Hood's fiction contains the same stark moral contrasts and unforgiving consequences that appear in O'Connor's writing, yet her narrative seems more often to remind the reader of the weight of circumstances, accidents, and misunderstandings as they affect human behavior. The orthodox quality of O'Connor's religious faith is replaced by a greater tolerance and a greater emphasis on the possibility of self-improvement. Nonetheless, there is in Hood's fiction an identical sense that the regional failure, in all of the different forms that it can be imagined, is an opportunity for redemption that is somehow lacking in more secular and materialistic cultures. Poverty and hardship are opportunities for human heroism and self-sacrifice, if also for divine grace.

In the writing of James Agee, the sense of regional failure is as pronounced as in any other writer, but there seems to be no salvation, no fortunate fall. Quite the contrary, Agee seems unable to resist the force of philosophical skepticism, and much of his career was spent in an effort to undermine the belief system that he associated with the bourgeois perspective of his mother's family. In the absence of this belief system, Agee struggled to establish a basis of faith on grounds ranging from social reform to Jungian analysis, but in the end none of these convictions was as compelling as Agee's overriding sense of nihilism. Agee's writing clearly reflects the influence of agnosticism, relativism, and libertarianism, positions that he discussed and espoused at various points, but his awareness of the inadequacy of these forms of skepticism caused Agee toward the end of his life to disavow all positions: finally, his imagination focused only on annihilation.

Influenced by the same cultural and philosophical forces, writers from the American South and the Caribbean have responded to a similar sense of spiritual crisis by exploring their relation to ethical traditions and attempting to regain a stable basis for belief. From a perspective outside the cosmopolitan centers of modern culture, these writers are able to recognize the limitations of an ethics that is based on little more than a closed-minded and reflexive opposition to all purposeful conceptions of existence. Refusing to make judgments of any kind, the philosophy of radical skepticism is a withdrawal from life that relegates society to an anarchic condition ruled by self-interest alone. In response to this damage, southern and Caribbean writers from Faulkner to Naipaul have sought, in Naipaul's words, "a more direct, less unprejudiced way of looking" (*Enigma* 142)—"less unprejudiced" in that they admit the necessity of writing from the perspective of a particular ethical tradition and, because of this fact, of having to judge the damaged world in which they live, not merely record it from a safe distance. Reflecting on the destructive consequences of philosophical skepticism, these writers have begun to search beyond the culture of doubt and suspicion for a workable tradition of belief. Theirs has been a fearful journey through a century of psychic pain, social upheaval, horrific violence, and doubt as to the very right of human beings to exist.

Speaking of such trauma, Canetti offered a chilling warning. "One survives so much," he wrote in *The Human Province*, "that one mistakenly thinks one can survive anything" (77). In response to such threats to survival, the rediscovery of faith is culture's most important task, and the contribution of fiction writers to this enterprise is an exciting, inspiring, and demanding responsibility. With their reconsideration of the potential validity of inherited traditions of belief, a number of modern authors have explored those avenues of authority that in the past, as Hannah Arendt writes, "gave the world the permanence and durability which human beings need precisely because they are mortals" (*Portable* 465). In a century of unprecedented violence and alienation, writers of fiction from Faulkner to Naipaul have responded with the creation of a literature of conviction and belief.

1

Faulkner, Canetti, and Survival

Few writers have been so keenly aware of the damage of skepticism and moral indifference as William Faulkner and Elias Canetti. In his Nobel Prize acceptance address, speaking of the "fear so long sustained by now that we can even bear it" ("Address" 723), Faulkner alluded to the instinctive fear of violence that threatens to reduce human existence to a barbaric world of threat and counterthreat. In such a world, with its absence of humanizing traditions and shared beliefs, prejudice and mistrust are the controlling motives for human action, and society is ruled by force rather than by the power of reason or the rule of law. In such circumstances, there is no room for loyalty or selflessness, and it is always the weak who suffer the most. As Faulkner makes abundantly clear in his Nobel address, the potential for society to devolve into brutish anarchy is always present, yet he "refuses to accept" this vision of life. In asserting that "man will not merely endure: he will prevail," Faulkner is pointing to the distinction between mere physical survival and a civilized conduct of life based on understanding and compassion and defended by courageous action. Mankind's "immortality" is grounded not merely in the ability to survive physically but, more importantly, in the possession of "a spirit capable of compassion and sacrifice and endurance" ("Address" 724).

In transcending the instinctive level of fear, human beings reach toward a more enlightened state of forgiveness and hope, but in order to reach this condition of "prevailing," they need to grasp the destructive potential of mistrust, egotism, and greed, instincts rooted in a deep-seated anxiety concerning survival that too often control human relationships. The power of these destructive instincts can only be restrained by the influence of faith and reason, and this restraining influence depends, to a large extent, on the vitality of those traditions and institutions whose purpose it is to transmit stabilizing models of order and belief from one generation to the next. As Faulkner stressed in his Nobel Prize speech, the writer contributes to this process of cultural continuity through a fearless and self-sacrificing, if not exactly "selfless," dedication to the telling of "the old universal truths." Faulkner insists that man "is immortal...because he has a soul, a spirit capable of compassion and sacrifice and endurance" ("Address" 724), though these sentiments must be tempered by Faulkner's recognition that, in the words of Isaac McCaslin, "man made a heap of his circumstances, him and his living neighbors between them" ("Delta" 646). Yet Isaac's less than sanguine words are themselves contradicted by his final gesture of passing along General Compson's hunting horn, his most precious inheritance, to the child of Roth Edmonds and his cousin, an African American descendant of James Beauchamp. For once, Isaac's action is selfless and courageous.

A similar vision of the development from the instinctive level of violence and fear to a humane concern for others is apparent in the writing of one of William Faulkner's major contemporaries, Elias Canetti. Although there is no evidence of mutual influence, indeed, no indication in their published works, letters, or public statements that Faulkner and Canetti were familiar with one another's writing, the two authors would find their works shaped by the same historical crises—two world wars, a global depression, the rise of totalitarianism, and the Holocaust. In their response to these horrific events, Faulkner and Canetti brought to bear similar cultural resources, among which were an intricate knowledge of Judeo-Christian and classical mythic narrative and a profound respect for Western institutions of law and government. During a period in which they saw tens of millions of human lives sacrificed to the political extremism of fascism, Stalinism, and other factions, Faulkner and Canetti were moved nearly to despair, but they worked beyond their despair to fashion new ways of understanding man's relationship to the past and to the inherited institutions and beliefs that are the legacy of past generations. In the end, Faulkner and Canetti arrived at similar conclusions concerning the innate propensity of human beings toward violence, and in response each writer produced a conception of art as a corrective to the destructive tendencies of human society.

Elias Canetti, born in 1905, just eight years after William Faulkner, won the Nobel Prize for Literature in 1981, thirty-two years after Faulkner received the award. Canetti's only novel, *Die Blendung* (translated as *Auto-da-Fé* in 1946) was published in 1936, and his two major dramatic works, *Hochzeit* (*The Wedding*) and *Die Komödie der Eitelkeit* (*Comedy of Vanity*) were written in the early 1930s (though, in part for political reasons, not published or produced until after World War II), the same years in which Faulkner completed *Light in August, Absalom, Absalom!*, and other major works. Canetti's crowd theory, itself only part of his wide-ranging research and creative activity, is elaborated in his monumental work, *Masse und Macht* (translated as *Crowds and Power*) published in 1960 but the product of over three decades of research begun amid the unfolding Nazi terror of the 1930s and the 1940s. During this same period of crisis, Faulkner's writing shifted from the more regional and autobiographical basis of his early novels to an increasing political concern, a more "public" side of his work that was developed in novels such as *Go Down, Moses* and *Intruder in the Dust* and that culminated in the publication of *A Fable*, the presentation of his Nobel acceptance speech, and his role as a cultural representative of the United States during the 1950s.

It was perhaps predictable that, having lived through the most brutal and anarchic decades in human history, both Faulkner and Canetti would first seek to understand the cause of the horrific events that they had witnessed. They discovered the cause in an unrestrained millennialistic culture originating in the Enlightenment dream of human perfectibility, and in response to this unraveling of culture, they urged a return to more stable traditions and institutions of human civilization. Canetti's social theory, far more complex than that of his predecessor Gustave Le Bon,[1] sought to reaffirm cultural order by engaging in an encyclopedic reading in comparative anthropology, religion, myth, literature, and history, accompanied by an astute commentary that implied the necessity of restraint and mental order. Canetti's theory of social interaction is devoted to a struggle against the spread of authoritarianism of the sort that is connected with a universal anxiety concerning survival that Canetti represents metaphorically simply as "Death" (*Crowds* 162). It is this figure that turns a peaceful political gathering into a murderous mob or that leads to the concentration of power in the hands of a few. For Canetti, the anxiety concerning survival explains the reduction of art and beauty to propaganda or the transformation of healthy social contact into fear. The most significant part of Canetti's study is his examination of the "survivor": the figure of authority who imagines himself to be the "last survivor" of a crowd of dead subjects. Canetti analyzes the mechanisms of power involved in survivorship and how it functions through commands and symbolic discourse in relation to those ruled.

As Roger Kimball notes, Canetti was one of a number of twentieth-century intellectuals, including Max Weber, Hannah Arendt, and Hermann Broch, "fascinated by the spectacle of mass society—its expression in modern democracies and its perversion in totalitarianism" (27). In her classic study, *The Origins of Totalitarianism*, Arendt analyzed the process by which the individual within the totalitarianism system is stripped of all legal rights and, indeed, of identity itself. The natural inclination of totalitarian leaders toward violence is closely tied to this assault upon individuality, and the concentration camp is, in this sense, the logical outcome of totalitarian politics, for in the concentration camp the whereabouts of the individual is lost and everything, finally survival itself, is taken away. In the camps, as Arendt puts it, the prisoner's "death merely set a seal on the fact that he had never really existed" (133).

In Canetti's view, one that is also rooted in the author's reflection on the horrific practices of totalitarian regimes, modern society preserves its instinctive motives beneath the veneer of "civilization." The legal process of execution, for example, duplicates, in a less public forum, the death sentence carried out publicly in ancient societies. The electoral process, with its rituals of nominating conventions, parades, rallies, and celebrations, replicates tribal behavior in the selection and installation of chiefs. Modern warfare, despite its technological "advances," preserves many of the instincts of command, morale, and crowd cohesion familiar in primitive war parties. It is impossible to eliminate such deeply embedded instincts as those associated with mass meetings or the fear of crowds of enemies, but it is possible to understand, and eventually to control, these instincts. Yet, the potential for violence that Canetti explores in crowd psychology presents us with a chilling sense of mankind's potential for evil and with an awareness of an urgent need to restrain it.

At least three important elements of Canetti's work are anticipated in Faulkner's writing: the psychic imagining of crowds in relation to the self, the awareness of instinctive motives behind ostensibly "civilized" behavior, and the interest in the figure of "the survivor." Moreover, each of these elements can be traced to a single source: the complex relation to power that exists in all human beings. As Canetti shows, from childhood all human beings live under the burden of authority, beginning with the control of parents but soon extending to that of teachers, colleagues, employers, and others. When this authority is abused, the effect is to produce a form of anxiety under which human beings accumulate "stings." All members of society feel themselves to be burdened with command, and all instinctively attempt to evade the burden of command or to "pass along" to others the stings that they accumulate. One of the major functions of religion and art is to provide a mythic narrative of belief by means of which these burdens are assuaged and mitigated. For some, however, this proves impossible, and for these unfortunate members of society the burden of command results in a condition of schizophrenia.

There are several prominent examples of this condition in the novels of William Faulkner: the character of Darl Bundren in *As I Lay Dying*, Quentin Compson in *The Sound and the Fury*, and Gail Hightower and Joe Christmas in *Light in August*. At his window, ceaselessly memorializing the site of his grandfather's death, Gail Hightower embodies Canetti's condition of command, a "negativism" implied in the characteristic state of "a sentry standing motionless on guard for hours" (*Crowds* 311). In this condition, Canetti writes, the sentry "suppresses in himself all the fleeting impulses to activity, such as desire, fear or restlessness, of which human life mainly consists; and he fights them best by not admitting them even to himself" (311–12). This catalog of "prohibitions" seems a remarkably accurate description of Hightower's psychic condition, and it is, Canetti stresses, a condition that the schizophrenic comes to defend at all costs, for it is at once the basis of his identity and a defense against the threatening chaos of life. As Hightower realizes, thinking of the effect of his grandfather's memory, "I am the instrument of someone outside myself" (*Light* 491).

Nearly everyone in Yoknapatawpha is burdened by the past and often, more specifically, by what Canetti refers to as "the resentment of the dead" (*Crowds* 262). As Byron Bunch, the comic hero of *Light in August*, expresses it: "A man will talk about how he'd like to escape from living folks. But it's the dead folks that do him the damage" (75). The fear of the dead, as Canetti points out, is a universal element in human religious belief, and the simple fact that the living have survived the dead is reason enough for this fear. To protect themselves from the damage that the dead can wreak, the living have developed rituals involving the offering of respect, gifts of food, and even human sacrifice. Through such rituals, the dangerous presence of the spirits of the dead is felt to be offset to some extent by continued worship or propitiation.

Hightower, of course, participates in his own less than efficacious form of ancestor worship. One of his earliest memories is the discovery, at age eight, of his grandfather's frock coat worn in the Civil War, and, beginning with this sacred relic, Hightower constructs a deadening psychological relationship to the past that involves immense pride in his grandfather's valor, and shame and guilt at his own survival. Hightower's grandfather was, in fact, hardly a heroic figure, a fact that his death made clear: as a member of Van Dorn's cavalry, the grandfather was killed not in a raid on Grant's stores itself but in the inglorious aftermath—in a henhouse while stealing chickens. As is evident in the mythological figure that his grandson creates, a reckless hero who inspires admiration by a disregard for his own safety as much as by his valor in combat, the grandfather is a thoroughly ironic figure, and Faulkner's attitude toward the mythology of the Lost Cause is, at this point in his career at least, skeptical, to say the least.

The narrative of Gail Hightower, from his lonely childhood obsession with the memory of his grandfather's "heroism" to his unfortunate marriage, fraudulent ministry, and long exile on the very street where his grandfather died, may be Faulkner's most convincing refutation of the Lost Cause mythology, yet Faulkner's perspective on military valor was never so cynical as was that of many of his contemporaries. Despite their seemingly obligatory performance of modernist exhaustion, Faulkner's early war stories, from "Ad Astra" and "Victory" to "All the Dead Pilots," preserve a good deal of respect for the combatants and for the motives of duty and honor that have brought them into conflict, even if, like Bayard Sartoris, they become absurdly fatalistic in response to the inhuman circumstances of war.

Nonetheless, Hightower's defensive obsession with his grandfather's death may be read as Faulkner's parable of mankind's enslavement to an instinctive psychology of violence, and of its long expiation and ultimate hope of transcendence. Near the end of the novel, Hightower reflects on heaven, "filled with...all the living who ever lived" (*Light* 492)—an apparent attempt to transcend his burdened condition—but, as we see in his fixated return to the memory of his grandfather's cavalry charge, Hightower never really resolves the dilemma of free will that his ancestor's death poses. Under slightly different circumstances, Hightower imagines, his grandfather's sacrifice might be fully comprehensible as part of a heroic victory; it might be cleansed of the accidental and inconsequential aspects of history and made invulnerable to the ravages of time and memory.

Hightower feels the need of this sort of monumentalizing because, as a "successor" who, as he imagines, will never experience anything of real consequence or achieve legendary status of any kind, Hightower feels despair in his own life and disdain for his father's bleak fatalism. To understand Hightower's obsession with his grandfather, it is necessary to consider his relationship to a father who is himself an unfortunate successor filled with a sense of worthlessness and uncertainty concerning his own right to exist. An intense anxiety about "time," which may be understood as anxiety about survival itself, is part of the frontier inheritance of Hightower, McEachern, Doc Hines, and others in the novel. In Hightower's case, his father, at age thirty "a man of spartan sobriety beyond his years" (*Light* 472), has been consumed by an obsessive focus on survival. The father's sheer drive and narrow ambition are "some throwback to the austere and not dim times not so long passed, when a man in that country had little of himself to waste and little time to do it in" (473). What Hightower fails to understand—and what his untutored friend, Byron Bunch, comprehends so well—is the role that his own loss of faith plays in his destiny. From childhood, Hightower views himself in fatalistic terms as a hopeless successor, two generations removed from the historic events that forever changed southern history. Because he was born too late, he is doomed from the start to reenact the mythic events of the past but never to participate in them. As a Civil War reenactor, so to speak, Hightower is condemned to permanent irrelevance.

Hightower's failure, then, cannot be understood as simply a consequence of his obsession with the past; rather, it is the wrong sort of obsession. In a manner not unlike the great artists/priests of modernism, he constructs what amounts to a private mythology that bears no authentic relationship to his civilization's enduring traditions of belief. His obsession with Civil War history is an attempt to fill the void created by modernity's cynical jettisoning of all workable tradition. In the place of a compelling tradition of faith, it inserts a mere fixation that is the product of a willful and alienated personality.

Hightower's willfulness is especially apparent in his unsympathetic relationship to his father. However unapproachable this father may have been—and for whatever reasons—Hightower's complete emotional separation from him is the decisive influence on his future life. In this respect, Hightower should not be seen as an eccentric case of rebellion but as a representative figure of modern alienation from authority. Like Joe Christmas, his psychic double in the novel, Hightower holds himself aloof from society in order to avoid participation in a rigid structure of paternal authority, but in doing so he relinquishes his identity. Hightower is as shapeless and impotent psychologically as he is physically. Like Christmas, Hightower's determination to live outside conventional expectations marks him as a heretic and a scapegoat. Implicitly, the entire course of his life is an attack on those forms of tradition and authority that society finds necessary to survival, so it is not surprising that the town should treat him as a pariah.

What Faulkner underscores in his creation of Hightower and Christmas is the destructive potential ever present in both the paternal relationship itself and in its disruption. In a sense, of course, the relationship of parents and children always involves the potential for inequity and abuse, but the conspiratorial manner in which the relationship is regarded in modern culture creates its own resulting sense of absence and futility. As Canetti has it, "All questioning is a forcible intrusion" (*Crowds* 284), and it should be obvious that the relationship between Joe Christmas and his stepfather, McEachern, is based on the exercise of such "force," as was the cold indifference of Hightower's relationship to his father. The nature of Joe Christmas' proposed induction into the church, through the study of the Presbyterian catechism, is based on a ritual of question-and-answer in which the initiate offers himself up to the power of the church and, by implication, to the control of the paternalistic culture that it represents. Against the force of such interrogation, Canetti identifies several forms of defense: silence, evasion, or the "possession of a secret" (*Crowds* 286), all of which Joe Christmas attempts to utilize. The rules of civilized discourse prohibit certain questions and certain forms of questioning, especially among strangers, yet in the belief that he serves God's wishes, McEachern violates all such codes of privacy.

McEachern's Calvinism, of course, stresses the belief in predestination and human corruption, theological conceptions that we may associate with a deep-seated and universal anxiety concerning survival. Canetti distinguishes Calvinism (and Islam) as religions based on the conception of divine "force" rather than "power." For believers of this kind, as Canetti writes, "The state of continuous expectation of command, to which, early in life, they surrender themselves for good and all, marks them deeply and also has a momentous effect on their attitude to other people. It creates a soldierly type of believer, men to whom battle is the truest representative of life" (*Crowds* 282). Because of the extreme form of Calvinism that he practices, McEachern demands a sort of spotlessness not only of himself but of everyone around him and particularly of those in his immediate family. While this self-righteous demand elicits submission from his wife, it provokes rebellion on the part of his adopted son, and yet, paradoxically, Christmas' rebellion against his rigid upbringing takes on a form that replicates Calvinism in many respects. The more that he devotes himself to the sinful ways of drinking, dancing, and whoring as part of his rebellion, the more Christmas comes to feel his own abhorrence of these forms of behavior.

Characteristically, Joe Christmas responds with silence to his stepfather's intrusive questioning, but, as Canetti shows, silence is a crude and ultimately ineffectual defense because it isolates the individual not only from others but from the resources of trust and belief. Christmas' tragic death results in large part from the fact that he can neither evade the rigid structures of order of his fundamentalist society nor adapt to them in the way that others such as Byron Bunch are capable of doing. In his fierce resistance to all forms of authority, Christmas rejects not only the excesses of his society but the possibility of love and trust altogether. He becomes alien in the deepest sense, to the extent that his bearing and facial expression mark him as "foreign" to the townspeople of Jefferson even before he speaks.

One of the main reasons for Joe Christmas' isolation is his immense distrust of women. From infancy his experience has contributed to his sense of abandonment and betrayal. As a result, his suspicion of women separates him from the sort of emotional healing that a stable domestic relationship might afford, and Joanna Burden's shifting emotional demands simply reinforce the strong suspicion of women that he already carries. Clearly, Joe's mental life is dominated by a defensive resistance to all who would attempt to restore him to the bonds of society that originate, as Canetti points out, in the figure of the mother that "is the core and very heart of" the institution of the family. The mother's nourishment and protection is an "activity [that] continues in a less concentrated form throughout many years" (*Crowds* 221).

The linkage of food and power, so much connected with the relationship of Joe to women in Faulkner's novel, is a concept that Canetti refers to as "the domestication of command" (*Crowds* 307). In his distrust of others, and particularly of women, Joe uncovers this ambivalent aspect of family life, one that involves sources of command that are generally obscured within everyday social transactions. "Everything which is eaten is the food of power" (219), Canetti writes in a section of *Crowds and Power* entitled "On the Psychology of Eating." The relationship of mother and infant involves more than nourishment and protection of the child, for in this role the mother's complete control of food "gives rise to a feeling of superiority greater than that obtaining in any other habitual relationship between human beings" (221). Joe Christmas instinctively comprehends the element of power that underlies the control and apportioning of food. To be dependent to any extent on another for food, as he is on the dietician at the orphanage, on Mrs. McEachern, on Bobbie Allen, on Joanna Burden, and even on the unassuming Byron Bunch, who offers his lunch bucket to the newcomer at the planing mill, reinforces the fear of abandonment and extinction that he has apparently carried with him from earliest childhood. This dependence is one of the reasons why Joe Christmas believes that women such as Mrs. McEachern are "unreliable" and manipulative in their kindness and why he prefers the "predictable" harshness of males (*Light* 159). Both Faulkner and Canetti, it would seem, recognize that women participate in society as both victims and oppressors: in the case of Mrs. McEachern, the "screw of graying hair" (*Light* 165), a feature that she shares with Mrs. Armstid, identifies her as a victim of life's harsh injustice, "a patient, beaten creature" (165), but, like every human being, she in fact retains an instinctive need to assert control, if only over the feelings of a vulnerable eight-year-old orphan.

What is missing in Christmas' relationship with women is supplied in Byron's unconditional love for Lena Grove. Even with knowledge that Lena is the unmarried mistress of Lucas Burch and that Lena still intends to reunite with Lucas, even at the expense of Byron himself, who provides protection for her both before and after the birth of her child, Byron extends a selfless and uncalculating love, a love that by the end of the novel Lena shows signs of reciprocating. Drawing on an unarticulated mythical belief in Lena's need and his own obligation to protect the weak, Byron creates goodness out of nothing—and this despite his physical weakness, inexperience, and age. Because of his unspoken but secure recognition of the human condition, Byron acts correctly, if not always confidently, at each step in his relationship with Lena. Even though Lena has violated the town's sexual mores and Byron has exhibited unexpected independence of thinking in response to both Lena and Joe Christmas, one imagines that Byron and Lena will eventually marry and return to Jefferson or a similar locale, where they will rejoin society as pillars of respectability. Their love evinces a redeeming and transforming influence even on those who have shown little recognition of the limitations of the town's reflexive morality.

In contrast, Christmas' secretive relationship with Joanna Burden leaves them beyond the influence of the mythical realities that guide Byron and Lena's redeeming love. The brutish physicality of their sexual relationship leaves no room for emotional or spiritual niceties, and Christmas' defensive separateness is matched by Joanna's domineering control. One of the key points about their relationship is the process by which Joanna attempts to "domesticate" Christmas through the use of food, and the violent reaction of Christmas once he realizes how determined Joanna is to carry out her plan for his future. Canetti points to the ritualistic importance of the act of humans eating together, the "esteem for each other [that] is clearly evident in all who eat together" (*Crowds* 220). Those who refuse to eat in the company of others, such as Joe Christmas, "renounce" the mutual esteem and power of belonging to the group that the ritual act of communion entails. Christmas' insistence on eating alone creates an uneasy, mistrustful relationship with the other men at the planing mill just as his dining alone in the Burden house marks him as an outcast similar to Joanna Burden.

In the extraordinary language of Faulkner's narrator, Christmas' final action of returning to Mottstown, where he is captured, fulfills his plan "to passively commit suicide" (*Light* 443), a phrase that, intentionally or not, might well refer not only to his return to Jefferson but, more broadly, to his entire career of silence and isolation. It is not just the role of the conventional scapegoat that Joe Christmas enacts, however, but a peculiarly modern will-to-suicide connected with the novel's "wheel" symbolism that signifies a deterministic and reductive philosophy of radical skepticism. In his rejection of all inherited traditions and sources of authority, Christmas takes on the role of the radical skeptic, intent on undermining all inherited values and beliefs.

The most important link to society that Christmas rejects is that of the Protestant faith that dominates the South. In the regional culture that Faulkner records in *Light in August* and other novels, the church is the site where the townspeople engage in an impassioned enactment of survival. The central ritual of the Eucharist is a mythic dramatization of the relationship of the Christian community to a scapegoat figure whose sacrifice releases a powerful emotion of grief and at the same time anneals the collective burden associated with suffering and loss. It is fitting that Hightower, who, more than anyone else, has occupied the pulpit, should explicate the role of the church in the psychic drama of the town as he does on the night before Joe Christmas' death. As he listens to the music from the Sunday evening service, the secret message within this Protestant music, Hightower finds, is the sound of death, "the apotheosis of his own history" (*Light* 368)—a history that includes "brawling" but also courage, pride, and pleasure.

In his treatment of southern religion, Faulkner asserts a distinctly sardonic point of view, particularly in the early period of his writing. Violence, the "*crucifixion of themselves and one another*" (*Light* 368), is the southern people's escape from the intolerable burden of their harsh lives—shaped as their lives have been by the brutal legacy of the frontier—and their churches are the primary site for its symbolic enactment. Christianity itself, as Canetti understood it, is a "religion of lament" that is compelling because through its ritual "the hunting or baiting pack expiates its guilt by becoming a lamenting pack" (*Crowds* 145). Since this ritual frees men from the guilt attached to the actual or fantasized violence of their society, "religions of lament will continue to be indispensable to the psychic economy of men for as long as they remain unable to renounce pack killing" (*Crowds* 145). Just so, the town's collective participation, and satisfaction, in the killing of Joe Christmas produces a memory of violence and guilt that must be expiated, as Faulkner suggests in describing Joe Christmas' death as "soaring into their memories forever and ever" (*Light* 465).

Paradoxically, Joe Christmas' killer, Percy Grimm, is another scapegoat figure who is a product of the same type of social determinism: burdened from having been born "too late" to gain glory in World War I, Grimm engages in a desperate quest to confirm his manhood through his role as a member of the National Guard. The relationship of Percy Grimm to Joe Christmas is clarified by Canetti's understanding that the executioner is, in fact, another victim of "stings" and one who is under the same state of command as the sentry. The difference lies in the fact that the executioner, by virtue of the dual relationship to power (as both victim and victimizer), has the ability to rid himself of the sting of command: "An executioner passes on exactly what has been imposed on him" (*Crowds* 330).

The excesses of Calvinism that are partly responsible for Christmas' death are unfortunately matched by those of racism, and in *Light in August* Faulkner offers an exacting analysis of the destructive power of racial myths. As Canetti interprets it, "judgement is a disease": "Man has a profound need to arrange and re-arrange in groups all the human beings he knows or can imagine; by dividing that loose, amorphous mass into two opposing groups he gives it a kind of density" (*Crowds* 297). The need to impose this kind of "density" on everyday experience is felt especially by those like Doc Hines who seem to carry an intolerable burden of psychological slights and who, for various reasons, seem incapable of dealing with them.

Motivated by a fanatical terror of racial disempowerment and of women's reproductive capacity that seems to be grounded ultimately in his own fear of death, Doc Hines becomes a fanatical tyrant who cannot see beyond his own racism and misogyny. Doc Hines' murderous reaction to his daughter's sexuality and to the supposed racially mixed parentage of his grandson needs to be understood as the response of a paranoiac to forms of vitality that appear to threaten his continued dominance. The violent defensiveness of the paranoiac is directed against all others who would challenge his power and, in extreme cases, against all who, merely by virtue of their existence, seem capable of outliving him. In an analysis that may help to explain Doc Hines' irrational violence toward both his daughter and his grandson, Canetti writes that "the paranoiac type of ruler" strives "to keep danger away from his person" (*Crowds* 231) by means of executions rather than of confrontation. Survival becomes the "prerogative" of the ruler who is naturally hostile to survivors, including his successors. "The intensest feeling for power is that found in a ruler who *wants no son*" (*Crowds* 245).

Canetti's study of paranoia in the case of Daniel Paul Schreber is especially useful in understanding the character of Doc Hines. During the seven years of his institutionalization, Schreber recorded in great detail the "delusional system" of a paranoiac, a record that was later published in his *Memoirs of My Nervous Illness* (1903). Most important in this system is that for the paranoiac "there is always an exalted position to defend and make secure" (*Crowds* 436). Schreber imagines all of creation as an extension of his own body, to the degree that he "swallows" all creation so that all other creatures disappear and Schreber is "*the only man left alive*" (*Crowds* 442). The paranoiac is also an astute observer of crowds and one for whom words take on the greatest importance, especially in the way that they point toward "causal relations" (*Crowds* 452). As in Doc Hines' conviction about his grandson's racial identity, unmasking the "true" nature of relations becomes a mania for the paranoiac who develops a preoccupation with "acts of *recognition*" (*Crowds* 456). Schreber and Doc Hines also share a similar sense of divine mission—to the point where both end up quite mad. As "a vessel in which the divine essence slowly collects" (*Crowds* 460), Schreber bizarrely wishes "to conserve his precious substance" by immobilizing himself, and he conceives of himself as a "national saint" (*Crowds* 460). It is a hopeful sign, at least, that most in Yoknapatawpha do not share Doc Hines' fanaticism. Underlying the fact that they view Doc and Mrs. Hines "as if they belonged to a different race, species" (*Light* 341) is a common-sense resistance on the town's part to a menacing psychological condition.

In their own ways, Faulkner and Canetti both offer a realistic assessment of the large role that aggression and fear play in human relationships, but both writers also provide some reason for hope. Crowd behavior is not by any means always destructive: the identification with the crowd is a social instinct that involves pleasure, emotional release, and a sense of equality, and in the physical contact and sense of solidarity with the mass, the individual finds relief from the burden of "stings" passed down through social authority. The processes of ritualistic and narrative performance that Canetti discusses—religious rites, communion rituals, trickster narratives, and ceremonies involving masks—are all examples of the means by which mythic understanding is reasserted in opposition to abuses of power. An attentive reading of Faulkner's fiction reveals that the South has suffered its own horrific abuses of power and that Faulkner was conscious of the need to control the anarchic tendencies of society both within his own region and within the larger world. The psychological, and often literal, separation of human beings into distinct crowds is a common feature of southern society, and the instinctive response of fear that accompanies these social divisions is to be found all too frequently in Faulkner's Yoknapatawpha. Faulkner's positioning of the Byron Bunch and Lena Grove narrative in opposition to that of Joe Christmas and Joanna Burden signals his conviction that, given the enduring force of essential human instincts of pity and love, a workable relationship to structures of authority and belief is possible.

Even Hightower, a character who has lived in his "dark house" (Faulkner's original title for *Light in August*) of fatalism and isolation, is reawakened to a sense of "triumph and pride" (*Light* 404) after delivering Lena's baby. The birth summons up, for a moment at least, Hightower's hopeful imagining of how Lena will repeople the earth from the very site of destruction and death, the aptly named Old Burden Place. By far the most important male representative of this life force, however, is Byron Bunch. As he saddles his mule to summon Hightower for Lena, Byron entertains a fantasy of having never met her, imagining his eternal escape from the attachments and responsibilities that now circumscribe his existence. It is as if he could simply step outside of what Canetti calls "the human province"—the "knowing" that all human beings accumulate in the course of their ordinary lives and the "memory" and burden of the past that they inherit at birth—and exist, like Joe Christmas or Gail Hightower, in solitary "freedom." Just as he is about to accomplish this sort of renunciation, or at least attempt it, by relinquishing Lena to her rightful husband-to-be, Lucas Burch, Byron looks back on the scene of his temptation that he believes he is leaving forever. The importance of Byron Bunch's backward gaze, painful though the gaze may be for Bryon, is that in opposition to the novel's many examples of obsessive or fearful gazes, it is decidedly creative and even transformative, for the mental process that accompanies Byron's backward glance is part of a rich imaginative inner life that rarely finds open expression—at the end of the novel he is still quietly "despairating" himself up to propose marriage to Lena—but that the narrative reveals through interior monologue. As Byron watches the train on which Burch is escaping, for example, he likens the "wall" of train to a dyke momentarily holding back "the world," and with the aid of this imaginative construction he now realizes for the first time that he is destined to live forever in the world of "time" and "hope." Although he is not successful in apprehending Lucas Burch, Byron, through his recognition of the value of life, *is* capable of transforming fear and suffering into courage and compassion.

This transformative force, the counterbalance to the primal fear and violence that Canetti documents at such length in *Crowds and Power*, is more generally revealed in Faulkner's fiction than one might suppose. Both Faulkner and Canetti would undoubtedly have viewed the war against fascism as the foremost struggle of their time. In "Delta Autumn," one recalls, Isaac McCaslin, Will Legate, and Roth Edmonds slip into a discussion of the dangers posed by Hitler's rise to power. When Roth cynically suggests that fascism will prevail, not only in Europe under Hitler but under a homegrown form of political extremism in America, Isaac—despite his limitations, Faulkner's closest representative in *Go Down Moses*—replies that America is strong enough to "cope with one Austrian paper-hanger, no matter what he will be calling himself" ("Delta" 638). Roth's futility is answered by Isaac's faith that, if necessary, civilized human beings will fight "to protect does and fawns" (639). As Isaac later insists: "most men are a little better than their circumstances give them a chance to be" (644).

Similarly, *Light in August* portrays at least some examples of human beings who act "better" than one might expect. As many critics have noted, *Light in August* begins and ends with the story of Lena Grove's pilgrimage, first from Alabama to Mississippi in search of her promised husband, and then from Mississippi to Tennessee—perhaps "just travelling" (495) as Byron insists and as the anonymous furniture dealer who relates the events believes—in the company of Byron Bunch and her newborn child. While Lena's movement may appear to be inconsequential, or at least inconclusive, its steady determination, supported by all whom Lena encounters, takes on a ritualistic quality that suggests a formal procession: in Canetti's terms a symbolic enactment of order and permanence. By her very presence in the novel, Lena reaffirms the possibilities of trust, love, and charity that have been brought into question by Faulkner's exploration of the darkest motives of domination and fear.

As a social philosopher but also as a novelist, a playwright, and an essayist, Elias Canetti understood the intricate workings of the artistic imagination in its efforts to respond to the terrible events of twentieth-century history. The analysis that Elias Canetti brought to the study of crowds and power resulted in a greater knowledge of the instinctive bases of social behavior and, through this knowledge, a more determined effort to change human attitudes toward sharing the world and its material and cultural resources with others. Like Canetti, William Faulkner spent a lifetime engaged in an effort to uncover the hidden realities of power, instinct, and fear within human society and to encourage humanity to transcend these destructive instincts through self-knowledge and courage. Implicitly, Faulkner called on his reader to see beyond the confines of prejudice and to explore a more positive basis of belief than could be found in the narrow attitudes of racial supremacy and extreme Calvinism. Inevitably, Faulkner would explore the cultural resources of his own past—more tolerate racial practices and more moderate forms of Christianity—as an antidote to the negative aspects of southern culture that his early fiction so vividly documented.

"Memory believes before knowing remembers" (*Light* 119), Faulkner writes of Joe Christmas' formative childhood experience at the orphanage. Faulkner's aphorism is clarified by Canetti's study of mankind's collective memory of the hidden instincts of fear grounded in a universal anxiety concerning survival. What all humans "believe" before "knowing" is the potential of violence and persecution for those who cannot withstand the burden of command. What we believe before knowing involves an instinctive awareness of the means by which human beings assert dominance and power over others in response to their secret fears of extinction. Like Faulkner, Canetti spent much of his life attempting to understand the destructive impact of mankind's ancient fears of violence and persecution, and like his older contemporary, Canetti searched for ways of transforming social existence into a more enlightened and compassionate condition.

Note

[1] In the first attempt at a scientific study of human crowds, Gustave Le Bon, a nineteenth-century French social scientist, developed a theory of crowd behavior that anticipated modern crowd studies. As Canetti would later do, Le Bon compared crowds to microbes, a social metaphor that, for nineteenth-century "scientific" theorists, implied a mysterious route of "contagion" as well as the phenomenal speed of crowd formation. Another important metaphor for crowd behavior was hypnosis. To Le Bon it seemed that the unconscious, irrational, and often violent actions of crowds could be explained by their members' abdication of rational control to the hypnotic suggestion of a stronger will. Indeed, the nineteenth-century conception of "great men" of history underlies much of Le Bon's theory, as he explicitly cites Napoleon as the "great man" capable of molding

crowds to his will. Le Bon finds that the mental life of the crowd requires, in a sense creates, its demagogic leadership. The "morality" of the crowd tends toward self-sacrifice: the habit of "servitude" that Le Bon assumes to exist in the masses requires its master. Impressed by big events and imbued with a religious sentiment, the crowd seeks an idol, "a god before everything else" (Le Bon 85).

2

Ethics Adrift: Faulkner's
If I Forget Thee, Jerusalem

Working from the awareness of instinctual fear and violence that he developed in *Light in August* during the mid- and late-1930s, Faulkner proceeded to create some of his greatest fiction, including *Absalom, Absalom!*, *Go Down, Moses*, and *The Hamlet*. Another novel written during the late 1930s was *If I Forget Thee, Jerusalem* (published in 1939 as *The Wild Palms*). In *If I Forget Thee, Jerusalem*, William Faulkner relates the parallel stories of two couples, one pursuing a dream of romantic love, the other struggling for physical survival after they are caught up in the great Mississippi River flood of 1927. Seduced by their image of ideal love, the first couple is led further and further away from the sheltering bonds of family, community, and traditional institutions; motivated by their need for security, the other couple seeks desperately to return to these same conditions of normalcy. As he relates the two stories, moving alternately from one to the other, taking into account the physical, psychological, and economic necessities to which human consciousness is always bound, Faulkner develops an understanding of the relationship of ethical existence to the condition of human beings within time, nature, and society.

The contrast between the two stories in *If I Forget Thee, Jerusalem* involves a distinction between different scales of value, one based on an alliance of romantic love and capitalism, the other on a precapitalist and traditional conception of existence. Faulkner views the dichotomy as an opposition between a deathly, artificial society and a life-giving connection with a tradition that takes into account the relationship of human beings to the physical world. In the "Wild Palms" sections, Faulkner's story centers on two young lovers who flee the impossible restraints of their world in search of absolute freedom but find themselves overwhelmed by the constraints of economics, physical nature, and the effects of their past actions—in essence, by the order of the necessity within which they and all human beings live. As in O. Henry's famous tale, "The Gift of the Magi," a story that may have influenced Faulkner's novel, the lovers are not so much "star-crossed," as Douglas Day would have it (113), as they are opportunistic: desperate to secure their ideal happiness, they sacrifice everything for love and end with nothing.

From the beginning, the appearance of Harry Wilbourne and Charlotte Rittenmeyer implies alienation and fatality. Their Gulf Coast landlord finds Harry suspect, attired as he is in "disreputable khaki" and "no hat in a region where even young people believed the summer sun to be fatal." He also notices Charlotte's "queer hard yellow eyes" and "drawn" skin and her attitude of "complete immobile abstraction from which even pain and terror are absent" (*Novels* 496). It is hardly accidental that, of the four major characters in the novel—indeed, of all characters in the book—Charlotte is the only one who dies, and the emplotment of her death is intimately connected with the novel's trope of death as ethical demise. Charlotte is "deathly" because of her inordinate pride and ambition, a conception of sin that can be traced to ancient Western ethical traditions that identify humility, loyalty, and selflessness as virtues and that proscribe arrogance and self-love as vices. What Daniel J. Singal views as her virtue of "nobly transcending the mundane," a contempt for the ordinary that qualifies her as the epitome of the "Modernist as aristocrat" (231), should be read as a nihilistic rejection of her family, her culture, and her past. Charlotte's movement is hardly an ascent toward a higher level of culture or a new religious synthesis; as Faulkner's pattern of imagery reveals, it is a descent into unfeeling barbarism, violence, and death.

Singal is correct in characterizing Charlotte as a modernist heroine, but this does not imply that she is a noble figure. Modernism itself was fatally infected with an arrogance toward ordinary humanity that all too often allied it with fascist politics. Indeed, modernism, at least in the uncompromising forms it took in the writing of Ezra Pound, Wyndham Lewis, Edmund Blunden, and the later writing of W. B. Yeats, was not so much aristocratic—as Singal would have us believe—as it was totalitarian in its implications. Rather than being redemptive in nature, Charlotte's determination to force all experience toward an ultimate goal of purity and freedom parallels the rise of fascism during the 1920s and 1930s. In an uncanny way, Charlotte's radical aesthetics resembles that of Emilio Marinetti, an ardent supporter of Mussolini and one of the founders of Italian Futurism. Marinetti advocated a harsh, antihumanistic style that prefigured the destruction of all existing civilization through the "hygiene" of global war. To a significant degree, Marinetti's aesthetic theory focused on the liberation of the individual from the restraints of conventional norms, an aspect of his art that accords with Charlotte's uncompromising insistence on total freedom from social bonds. Like Charlotte's striving toward an end point of history, Marinetti looked to a future in which Western culture would be supplanted by a radicalized culture emancipated from the prosaic institutions of church, marriage, and law as well as the repressive influence of social and artistic conventions.

If Charlotte and Harry are proudly defiant of bourgeois expectations, however, their pride takes on a distinctly modern form that ends not in the vengeful wrath of an Achilles or the soul-damning rebellion of a Miltonic Satan but in a sort of moral escapism that masks itself as idealism. Given what they believe to be the insufficiency of "ordinary" existence as lived by most men and women, they seek an idealized love as salvation from the commonplaceness of life. Charlotte insists that "it's got to be all honeymoon, always. Forever and ever, until one of us dies," while Harry believes that they must be "good enough, worthy enough" of a love that he compares to the grandeur of the ocean (*Novels* 551). To their way of thinking, the everyday tasks of husband and wife are part of the general mediocrity of human society, a mediocrity that undermines the "perfection" that they insist on. As, in the course of his novel, Faulkner unravels the dubious foundations of their idealism, he reveals that it is based on a radical alienation not only from society, with its obligations of family and labor that would interfere with their "perfect" love, but from all life, human and otherwise. Their ultimate goal is independence from physical existence itself, and in the end such a goal necessitates either their own deaths or the death of all life other than their own. The implication of their separateness is far greater than what might be thought of as the right to live undisturbed, "doing their own thing" outside the mores of society. Once such independence as theirs is claimed, it entails the destruction or enslavement of an ever-widening circle of others, a consequence that Faulkner only hints of but that we must imagine in the lives of Charlotte's husband, Francis, and her abandoned children, as well as those "victims" of Harry's incomplete medical education and of Charlotte's grotesque "art."

Their love is not only destructive but at least in one sense, unlike the ocean to which Harry compares it, artificial, for it is enacted entirely in secrecy, metaphorically closed off from the open and majestic flow of nature. By virtue of its admission that their goal is entirely personal and acquisitive, Charlotte's conception of love ("To get what you want as decently as you can, then keep it" [*Novels* 554]) at least has the virtue of being more forthright than Harry's naïve ocean metaphor. Her conception of "getting what you want" reflects the triumph of utilitarian and pragmatic thought in the modern age, but her language also involves a revealing ambiguity. "To *get* what you want" suggests a materialistic model to which even human love, ostensibly her ultimate value, is reduced. Alternatively, "to get what *you* want" implies, as well, a universe of isolated consumers, each motivated by nothing more than personal desire and with no basis for collective affiliation or aspiration. Contrary to Singal's finding that Faulkner "summoned up Charlotte to express his own values and beliefs" (227) and even that she represents "a form of female Christ" (238), there is convincing evidence to show that Faulkner intended Charlotte to be read as the most negative character in the novel and her influence on Harry to be viewed as ruinous.

Given the radical position that both Charlotte and Harry adopt, it is not surprising that their attempts at art are shown to be spurious and deadly productions. The "effigies" that Charlotte molds and that for a time support her and Harry are described as "elegant, bizarre, fantastic and perverse" (*Novels* 555). It is no wonder that they should sell well the first season that they are displayed but not at all afterward, for they are sensationalistic enough to catch the eye at first but can never provide the lasting satisfaction of true art. Charlotte herself refers to her creations as "[l]ike something created to live only in the pitch airless dark, like in a bank vault or maybe a poison swamp" (555–56). Her analogy suggestively connects her false art with the larger context of the novel in which a selfish and purely mercenary motive—one that recent critics have referred to merely as "capitalist" but that, in Faulkner's conception, represents a distinctively modern perversion of capitalism—ultimately controls Harry's and Charlotte's every act. Charlotte is hardly an "artist," for her creations express only alienation and defeat. In both her life and art, as Edmond L. Volpe notes, Charlotte exhibits a "selfish and immature perspective" that is "exclusive, warped, and life-negating" (71). When the effigies stop selling, Charlotte turns to creating puppets as photographic models for magazines and advertisements—a creation of grotesque parodies of Quixote, Falstaff, and other literary characters that Volpe terms "hate-filled versions" of their originals (70). With this as their livelihood, it is little wonder that Harry imagines their existence in pathetic terms, not only as inhuman but as that of creatures trained to perform at a circus with Charlotte balancing their lives "like a trained seal does its ball" (*Novels* 557).

For his part, Harry turns to the writing of lurid romance stories for confession magazines—just the sort of fraudulent models of behavior that the Tall Convict has so deeply resented. Harry's writing of false love is a reflection of his collapsing faith, for he tells Charlotte that "there is no place…in the world today" (*Novels* 587) for the sort of ideal love that they have attempted. What is not apparent to Harry is that he and Charlotte are *responsi-*

ble for the ruin in which they live and from which they suffer. In his cynicism Harry maintains that life is a swift progression from "*I was not*" to "*I am*, and time begins, retroactive, is was and will be. Then *I was* and so I am not and so time never existed" (588). In fact, as the Tall Convict knows quite well, time—despite its inescapable and precipitate movement—is the element in which life's abundance unfolds, bringing with it, in his case, more than he could imagine of hardship and pain but also of creation and love. At no point can we imagine his saying that "time never existed." On the other hand, Harry is not only cynical but, as his demeaning metaphor demonstrates, his relationship to Charlotte is based on a perverse self-deprecation, even to the point of envisioning himself as a sparrow, "the consort of a falcon" (591), and of imagining McCord and Charlotte as his "parents."

By contrast the Tall Convict and the country woman are immersed in and become agents of an environment which is, if anything, overly "natural" and productive. The Tall Convict, whose attitude toward life is characterized as a sort of "meditation" (*Novels* 594), engages in a more profound art than either Charlotte or Harry. In a storytelling of measured and laconic authority, he never escapes the deep-set reticence that is so much a part of the countryman's nature, but unlike the fraudulent creations of Charlotte and Harry, his telling is scrupulously honest and true. In the end, the Tall Convict demonstrates an impressive understanding of the purposefulness of the events that he describes, something that is not only absent but under attack in Charlotte's parodies of famous works of art. Furthermore, as Faulkner makes clear in his description of the effect of the Tall Convict's tales on his listeners, the convict's storytelling holds the attention of his listeners because of its authenticity, a moral certainty that is conveyed through his narrative's stark qualities of understatement and factuality.

What the Tall Convict comprehends about men and women reveals his keen intelligence at work, stripping away the shibboleth of romantic love to get at one of his civilization's foundational myths of human relationships. In doing do, he arrives at an understanding identical to the biblical view of gender as summarized by Vigen Guroian: "In the Bible's terms, the two whom God intended to be in intimate communion became divided into two opposing sexes. The complementarity of gender was corrupted, the communion was replaced by brokenness and separation, love by lust, and henceforth the sexes play out a deadly and demeaning game of lure and pursuit" (124). The Tall Convict is, of course, a Noah-figure intended to play his part in the redemptive history of mankind, and it is particularly in his effort to reestablish what Guroian refers to as "the complementarity of gender" that this purity is enacted. Volpe notes that "[t]he convict's apparent disdain for women is at least partially an act" (79), and, if we are to judge by his actions rather than his words, his attitude involves a depth of compassion and pity that is utterly lacking in Harry and Charlotte's relations. Looking upon the country woman's swelling body, the convict sees himself and her "equally" as "victims" of her condition, and his ceaseless determination during the course of their journey is to protect her and her child. Humorously, of course, the convict speaks of wishing to escape his responsibility: as the snakes slide out of the boat as it leaves the Indian mound, the woman's screaming unnerves him to the point that he cries: "Hush! I wish I was a snake so I could get out too!" (*Novels* 655). The point is that he does not "get out," nor does he ever seriously consider doing so, until he has delivered the woman, the baby, and the boat to the authorities who entrusted him with his mission.

In his determination to protect the weak, the Tall Convict exemplifies the most crucial of the "ultimate values" (23) that Cleanth Brooks points to in Faulkner's fiction. Whether in the example that Brooks cites from *The Unvanquished*, in the bumpkin heroism of Byron Bunch in *Light in August*, or in innumerable other examples, Faulkner writes repeatedly of "pity and love" as the central virtues of civilization as he conceives of it. We would do well to ponder the significance of this emphasis within Faulkner's ethics and its origin within a framework of Christian values, a view of Faulkner's work that has been partly reaffirmed but significantly qualified by later critics such as Janet Carey Eldred, who has characterized *Jerusalem* as a "*middle-class* Christian discourse" (149, emphasis added).

In an important and perceptive reading of *Jerusalem*, Cynthia Dobbs arrives at conclusions similar to those of Brooks concerning the nature of the cultural values represented in the novel, but she offers an opposing perspective on the viability of these values. Studying the connection between cultural discomfort with free-market capitalism in the 1930s and the "radical fluidity" also associated with women's bodies, Dobbs finds that Faulkner "calls into question the very idea of 'the natural'" (812) yet ultimately pulls back from this questioning to reinscribe the very same traditional conceptions of gender that he has previously brought into doubt. This seems to me an accurate summary, but Dobbs goes on to suggest that Faulkner's ethics is inherently flawed and, in its own way, "unnatural." This reading, especially Dobbs' view of the Tall Convict's desire to return to prison as "the longing to transcend, or entirely avoid, sexual desire itself" and the assertion that in its representation of prison labor the novel depicts "a sort of reliable, abstract, pure pleasure divorced from the insecure marketplace" (822–23), seems unconvincing, as does Dobbs' opinion that the convict's vision of the country woman as "a malevolent nature whose 'creative fluidity' is actually all about destruction" (821). Focusing almost exclusively on one aspect of the convict's characterization—his presumed "fear" of women—this reading fails to credit the bleak and subtle irony of his expression and his penchant for comic hyperbole, a quality of discourse that Faulkner identifies with the plain folk not only in this novel but also in *Sartoris, As I Lay Dying,* and *Light in August*. If we fail to look beyond the convict's words to the reality of his deeds, we risk an especially repugnant form of cultural arrogance—in this case, applying the standards of contemporary middle-class "correctness" to the rural and working-class values of an earlier time.

It is, of course, possible to engage, as Dobbs does, in reading from an altogether different epistemological perspective than the traditional conceptions of gender and class that I find implicit in Faulkner's novel. All structures of consciousness are to some extent the product of historical forces, and all inherited conceptions, such as the extreme reverence of motherhood that Faulkner relies on in rejecting Charlotte's example and affirming that of the country woman, are constantly though gradually reshaped in response to historical reality. Indeed, the limitation of critical approaches such as that of Dobbs lies precisely in the suggestion that there is a rational or "natural" alternative conception to pose in opposition to Faulkner's, a suggestion that underlies her ability to characterize the convict's perspective as "warped" (Dobbs 819), as an "odd romanticism" (821), and to label the representation of the country woman's femininity as "disturbing" (826). Since all epistemological systems are arbitrarily and historically constructed, there is no rational basis for either accepting or rejecting any particular tradition of belief. Dobbs' objection to what she takes to be a "conventional" (826) epistemology has no more objective validity than does the convict's position itself since any system of gender or class that would replace a "conventional" one would itself comprise yet another tradition, itself subject to rejection on other grounds. What does provide Faulkner's position, if we take it to be what Brooks proposes, with validity of a sort is that it is rooted in a longstanding ethical and religious tradition that has been embraced by a large majority of those living within Western civilization over the course of several thousand years. Like all traditions, the classical-Christian tradition that underlies Faulkner's writing provides its followers with a framework of belief essential to mental coherence and practical reasoning. While arbitrary in some sense, as a major tradition of belief it has remained relatively stable over time and necessarily so if it is to provide the basis for an ordered and meaningful life.

The psychological necessity of this conception of normalcy has been elucidated in detail by Alasdair MacIntyre, from whom my argument concerning historical traditions has been drawn. As MacIntyre writes, "One of the functions of the structures of normality is that by making it unnecessary for almost everybody all the time to provide justifications for what they are doing or are about to do, they relieve us of what would otherwise be an intolerable burden" (25). Should the particular historical tradition in which Faulkner writes be displaced by a different tradition, that new tradition would immediately prescribe its own conception of normalcy, and this conception would be perceived as natural and normal by most persons within the new tradition, a fact that Dobbs' analysis itself illustrates by its assumption that an alternative reading of gender and class proceeds from a more "truthful" conception of the female body and of economic relationships, understandings that contain their own implicit rules of normalcy.

The question of the validity of Faulkner's assumptions, then, is really a matter of one's perception of historical processes governing traditions and of changes in these processes since the period when Faulkner wrote, at which time we can assume that, given the critical and ultimate popular success of his fiction, his assumptions reflected a consensus among at least a segment of American and European readers. In what directions and to what extent Faulkner's tradition has been modified or whether it retains validity at all is a question of interpretation involving an assessment of the state and direction of contemporary culture, and this assessment is a matter of differing opinions. The problem is that a large number of such assessments *do* claim to have an objective basis beyond simple preference, and in this respect, claiming an authority that they do not actually possess, they rely on a misleading, and often coercive and authoritarian, rhetoric.

This is not to say that there are no grounds upon which to argue the preference of one tradition over another. As an individual shaped by a particular culture, I may happen to privilege pity and love above all other virtues, and like Brooks, I may find these virtues in Faulkner's work. Moreover, from within the classical-Christian tradition that has shaped my very rationality, I would trace their origin to what I view as the "nature of human existence," yet, from within a Buddhist or Hindu tradition, my understanding of the "nature of human existence" and my priority of values would be quite different. In fact, all arguments for the preference of one tradition over another are constructed from within the tradition with which one has been educated or aligned oneself, as is the tradition advanced in my own reading of Faulkner's novels. In reality, most human beings are never faced with the necessity of choosing one cultural tradition over another: they live out their lives firmly entrenched within one particular belief system. It is only a few who harbor the illusion that it is possible to choose freely among various ethical cultures, yet even where this might appear to be the case, it can be demonstrated that one is acting upon prior dispositions and training. Even more unfathomable is the notion that one can disengage from particular modes of rationality altogether: to float freely, moment by moment, among a countless number of ethical and cultural positions. In fact, it is impossible not to align oneself with a particular moral and philosophical tradition, even if this consists merely of the outworn Enlightenment assertion of free will.

Although Brooks' judgment of Faulkner's ultimate values seems to me convincing, his discussion does not clarify the *means* by which these values are tested and known. In Faulkner's imagination, the natural environment is the basis for knowing the human condition and its needs. Unlike Harry and Charlotte, the Tall Convict and the country woman are engulfed all along in an environment in which everything, especially the flooded rivers on which they are forced to live, seems to have sentience. Their relationship to nature supplies them with the deep understanding of life's purpose that Harry and Charlotte lack. Even when faced with the daunting task of hunting a large and dangerous creature that he has never encountered before (an alligator), the Tall Convict's mind works instinctively from an unerring knowledge of the physical world: the alligator is different from but not entirely unlike the mule that he has fitted with a halter or the hog with which he has wrestled. At another point, looking out on the surface of the Mississippi River, the convict compares it to "the color of a waffle or perhaps of the summer coat of a claybank horse" (*Novels* 664). Although they would know the waffle, not many readers today would be familiar with the claybank horse ("a horse of yellowish color"), a knowledge that affords the convict a means of relating the flooded river, colored as it is with soil and debris, to his known experience. The horse's coat also has "that same piled density" (664) as the river's surface. Perhaps the river is "horse-like" in other ways; certainly its "coat" is governed by the changing seasons in the way the horse's is. The knowledge of horses makes possible a richness of experience that the mere waffle reference would not.

In contrast with the immersion of the Tall Convict and the country woman within an abundant, fecund world of nature, Harry and Charlotte inhabit a wintry, isolated, sterile landscape, and, significantly, they inhabit this ghastly world by choice: in order to escape the commitments of labor and domesticity, they live on the fringes of established society where they must occupy out-of-season lake and Gulf Coast cabins and accept irregular and even fraudulent employment (Harry's appointment as a mine "doctor"). Like the bohemian artists on whom they model their lifestyle and like later-day bohemians of the 1960s, they choose freedom at all costs. Harry and Charlotte flee to further and further extremes in order to maintain their illusory independence. From New Orleans to Chicago, from Chicago to a freezing cabin in an abandoned Wisconsin lake resort, from there back to Chicago and then to a bankrupt mining camp in Utah, and finally, to a tourist cabin on the Gulf Coast, their progression mirrors the desperation with which they defend an idealized, fully abstract conception of being.

At various moments, Harry is conscious of how much they have sacrificed, as when, listening to a loon's voice on the Wisconsin lake, he thinks "how man alone of all creatures deliberately atrophies his natural senses" (*Novels* 566). Harry's comment reflects a clear recognition that physical nature is the touchstone of all human civilization and that, as human beings further isolate themselves from nature, they risk a fatal separation from spirituality and truth. Faulkner repeatedly voiced the same concern to his mother during his first years away from home, as when living in New Orleans, he wrote of rural Mississippi: "Golly, I miss the hills and fruit trees and things now. Think of all that grand country to walk and ride through, and yet folks will make their homes in a city!" (*Thinking of Home* 188). Chicago, the traditional urban *bête noire* of southern authors and certainly of Faulkner, is depicted as particularly unnatural in Faulkner's description of McCord's "upside-down day at the newspaper" (*Novels* 576) and Charlotte's work at window-dressing in a department store that at night takes on "a ruthless and infernal inverted life" (576), though seemingly nothing could be more infernal than the terms in which Faulkner evokes the store's *daytime* life: "the ruthless voracious murmur of furred shoppers and the fixed regimented grimaces of satin-clad robot-like saleswomen" (576).

"Ruthless": the urban department store is cruel and pitiless at *all* times because it is driven by the narrow values of consumer capitalism. Governed by nothing more than satisfaction of material desires, it is robotic, filled with manikins that simulate life, everywhere sterile and dehumanized. It is not coincidental that the two abortions that are performed in the novel are motivated by a similar consideration, the desire to preserve the greatest degree of personal autonomy within a capitalist system in which individuals seek "fulfillment" through consumption. Within this system, given the pressure to maintain a sense of independence in the service of self-expression and self-gratification, the cost of child-rearing is inevitably calculated in monetary terms as well as in the extent to which parenting limits personal freedom. It is precisely this calculation that is involved when Buckner, the mine manager, asks Harry to perform an abortion so that he and his wife can have what they believe to be "another chance" at happiness. Perversely, Charlotte urges Harry to perform the abortion by saying: "This is for love too. Not ours maybe. But love" (*Novels* 626).

The nexus between what Charlotte means by "love" and the economic necessity that governs her life is a crucial issue in Faulkner's novel. Since Faulkner himself was continually occupied by the problem of how to fund his artistic freedom in a world in which he was responsible for his dependents, it should come as no surprise that this concern finds its way into his writing. It is the burden of Faulkner's famous complaint to Robert Hass in a letter of 3 May 1940 in which he spoke of himself as "an artist...who should be free even of his own economic responsibilities" but who became the "sole, principal, and partial support" of at least seven others, in addition to inheriting his "father's debts" and "dependents, white and black" (*Selected Letters* 122). In the final analysis, however, Faulkner *did* fulfill his responsibilities toward his wife, Estelle, and the natural and adopted children in his household, for to do otherwise would have violated his ultimate values of pity and love.

Just as Faulkner recognized his responsibility in his own life, he applied the same standard of judgment to his characters, and it is on the basis of this moral standard that he judges Harry and Charlotte's relationship as "perverse." For one thing, Faulkner implies that his modern lovers violate a scheme of nature in which there exists a differentiation of gender roles grounded in the belief, axiomatic in Western thinking, that, since women give birth to and nurture children, men are expected to labor to support them. Hannah Arendt summarizes the classical conception of the mutual dependency of men and women: "That individual maintenance should be the task of the man and species survival the task of the woman was obvious, and both of these natural functions, the labor of man to provide nourishment and the labor of the woman in giving birth, were subject to the same urgency of life" (186). Harry and Charlotte violate this traditional conception of the household at their own risk. Given the disastrous result of their inversion of gender roles, Karen Ramsay Johnson's argument that in many of his novels Faulkner's transgression of gender is connected with a "re-creative process of narration" (1) hardly seems convincing. The pain brought about by Charlotte's abandonment of her two children, a decision necessitated by her radical quest for freedom, radiates throughout the narrative and thus undermines the conclusion that she and Harry have achieved the happiness they set out to find. Just the opposite: their transgression of convention leads them step by step toward a greater burden of guilt, pain, and self-doubt. As a rationale for not giving birth to another child, Charlotte complains that children "hurt too much" (*Novels* 642), suggesting that she has suffered from giving them up. It is a perverse and illogical train of thought for her then to insist on aborting the child that presumably she and Harry would not feel compelled to give up in order to continue living together. In fact, we may imagine that Charlotte's real reason for insisting on the abortion may be more prosaic: she does not want the everyday responsibility of child care to interfere with the ideal romance that she and Harry are attempting, unsuccessfully, to sustain. As Joseph R. Urgo writes, "The continuity of bodies, from mother to child, denies the autonomy of the female self, and the 'hurt' that Charlotte seeks to abort is the pain of this intrusive, unwelcome qualification of her own independence" (258).

In contrast with Harry and Charlotte's pursuit of autonomy, the Tall Convict is motivated by selfless values that require him to put the needs of others ahead of his own desires. Even in prison, his conduct reflects "his own honor in the doing of what was asked of him, his pride in being able to do it, no matter what it was" (*Novels* 607). So important is the distinction between the value of service to others and the destructive force of autonomy that the novel's structure of tropes centers on it: unlike the dwindling scale of Harry and Charlotte's world, which is bounded by the narrow walls of hotel rooms, cabins, cheap urban apartments, and finally a hospital room, the environment that the Tall Convict and the country woman inhabit is excessively large, and the Tall Convict, in responding to it, takes on dimension. After he is shot in the hand while trying to give himself up, he is compared to the "dying rabbit" with its scream "an indictment of all breath and its folly and suffering, its infinite capacity for folly and pain, which seems to be its only immortality" (613). This description reveals a fundamental and decisive paradox: the Tall Convict, accepting his earthly limitations as does the dying rabbit, nonetheless achieves "immortality," while Harry, aspiring to flight, if only that of the sparrow, conceives of existence as nothing more than a meaningless prelude to total annihilation. Accepting the folly and suffering that are his lot, the Tall Convict is "infinite," while Harry and Charlotte are ruined by their fear and weakness.

The nature of the country woman's heroism is more problematic, for she is the least developed of the major characters in the novel. This is important because she is, or ought to be, the character through whom Faulkner dramatizes his understanding of the nature of ethical life for women. Her lack of narrative development suggests a Faulknerian blind spot: while Faulkner demonstrates a clear sense of what is involved in heroism for men, he rarely dramatizes a white female engaged in heroic tasks. Of course, selfless devotion is often associated in Faulkner's work with black women such as Dilsey Gibson in *The Sound and the Fury* or Nancy Mannigoe in *Requiem for a Nun*, both of them latter-day "mammy" figures whose devoted care for their white families is the product of a history of servitude, and as such an unnatural and enforced heroism. For white women, the evidence of their sacrifices is clear enough, but they rarely take center stage as moral agents. Thus, Faulkner's characterization of the country woman betrays his inability to conceptualize the positive contribution of women in a *particularized* manner, but the traces of such a role are apparent in the treatment of this and other country women in his works. Within the context of the degraded modern culture that Faulkner presents in *Jerusalem*, characters such as these possess a vestigial consciousness of the more encompassing role that women must have performed in preindustrial Western civilization.

In contrast with the heroism of the Tall Convict and with that implicit in the character of the country woman, the failings of modern women, and men, are made explicit. Like Dante's adulterous lovers, Paulo and Francesca, Harry and Charlotte consider themselves servants of love who should be granted license freeing them from mundane responsibility. Given their tendency toward metaphoric, emotional, and physical "flight" and the nature of Dante's punishment for such airy abstraction, the dry wind rushing through the palms is the appropriate symbol of their sterile aspiration. That the dry wind sweeps through the particular scenes in which Harry performs an abortion upon his own lover is a significant extension of the metaphor, for it signals the totality of his and Charlotte's separation from nature, community, and tradition.

Faulkner's extraordinary evocation of the hospital where Charlotte dies has a special relevance to the theme of the novel. In a remarkable descriptive passage, the hospital corridors are pictured as "carbolised vacuums of linoleum and rubber soles like wombs into which human beings fled before something of suffering but mostly of terror, to surrender in little monastic cells all the burden of lust and desires and pride, even that of functional independence, to become as embryos for a time yet retaining still a little of the old incorrigible earthy corruption" (*Novels* 698). Because the hospital in question is receiving the dying body of Charlotte following an unsuccessful abortion, Faulkner's description marks a profound and climactic point of connection between the parallel stories in the novel. Unlike the Tall Convict, an adult who seeks independence but not freedom, and the country woman, an adult who seeks nurture for her child, Charlotte is figuratively an unborn child who enters a kind of "monastic" environment in which the residents are utterly dependent, even non-functioning creatures. Unlike the Tall Convict, who accepts terror as his element, Charlotte "flees" terror at the price of "lust" and "desires" and "pride." In this airless and artificial environment, only in death does Charlotte return to the condition of nature as, like the flooded river that the convict and woman have ridden, she undergoes "a collapsing of the entire body as undamned water collapses" (*Novels* 702).

In contrast to the condition of alienation that Charlotte and Harry have pursued to the end, the Tall Convict and the country woman wish only to escape from the actual flood waters on which they are whirled about and which represent their unbidden separation from the ordinary routines of everyday life. When their small boat temporarily comes to rest on an ancient Indian mound, the Tall Convict reflects on the virtue of solid earth, which, despite its unforgiving hardness and its demands on those who make their living from it, "did not snatch you violently out of all familiar knowing and sweep you thrall and impotent for days against any returning" (*Novels* 652). The values of earth are the opposite of sky and water; earth implies "familiar knowing," "potency," and "returning," qualities that are basic to the Tall Convict's scheme of values. He seeks only to give himself up and return to the prison farm where he can live among known codes and customs and where he can work productively and exercise his talents to the fullest extent possible under the circumstances. What underlies the Tall Convict's desire to return to the "safety" of Parchman is the profound need of all human beings for normalcy. The virtue that the Tall Convict finds in predictable routine, shared rules of conduct, and self-restraint are not a measure of his neurotic flight from life—or, as some would have it, from the threatening intrusion of the "female"—rather they are a necessary aspect of mental order within his inherited belief system.

What Faulkner implies with the Tall Convict's monklike prison existence is not the psychological abnormality of his character but the abnormality of modern existence from which he flees. Ironically, and humorously, Faulkner suggests that human relationships can never approach the depth of friendship that the Tall Convict has enjoyed with his mule, John Henry ("whose ways and habits he knew and respected and who knew his ways and habits so well that each of them could anticipate the other's very movements and intentions" [*Novels* 658]), but the Tall Convict at least brings the same expectation of respect and dignity to his dealings with other people, even if in the context of a more knowing world of southern politicians, bureaucrats, and technicians, these are not reciprocated. The closest that the convict comes to finding complete rapport with another human being is with the Cajun swamp-dweller with whom he shares the same harsh fate, seeking "just permission to endure and endure to buy air to feel and sun to drink for each's little while" (668). Significantly, their communication is wordless and, thus, in the context of modernity's linguistic estrangement, near perfect.

The question of the Tall Convict's possible feelings of intimacy for the country woman with whom he has spent a month in a small boat is related to his values of selflessness and respect for life. The Tall Convict's experience with his first "sweetheart," on whose behalf he has perhaps attempted the unsuccessful train robbery, has soured him on "female companionship" (*Novels* 725), as the plump convict puts it, but his intimacy with the country woman goes far beyond what any of his prison mates can imagine and, indeed, beyond what Harry and Charlotte experience in their months of physical passion. The country woman is a fellow human being who is completely dependent on the Tall Convict for her own and her child's survival. There is an unspoken communication between them with the understanding that he will provide all that is necessary, including, at last, their safe return to the sort of human society where her child can be nurtured, and this at the expense of his own reincarceration and the indignity of receiving ten years of additional sentence for "attempted escape." Their circumstances, which are, in fact, the circumstances of all human beings, elicit intimacy of the most profound sort, though one neither romantic nor sexual in nature.

Faulkner implies that the Tall Convict and the country woman share an intimacy that is not typical even, or especially, for married couples. The product of Faulkner's years in Hollywood, *If I Forget Thee, Jerusalem* was, after all, written during a period when Faulkner was separated for long periods of time from his wife, Estelle, and during which he was involved in an affair with Meta Carpenter. Clearly his doubts regarding the institution of marriage, if not about the more fundamental responsibilities of spousal and parental support, are evident in the novel. Faulkner equates "the old married" with "the thousand identical coupled faces" whose eyes express their lives of "disaster and alarm and baseless assurance and hope and incredible insensitivity and insulation from tomorrow" (*Novels* 667): in contrast with these worn marriages, it is hardly a conventional union that Faulkner has in mind in his portrayal of the convict and the country woman. Their relationship is enacted in the realm of necessity but is, at the same time, a communion of immortal souls, a woman of absolute loyalty and perseverance and a man of infallible integrity and strength.

In a thoughtful reading of the choices posed in the novel, Joseph Urgo finds that Faulkner's novel "compels us to recognize the Age of Abortion as one in which we must confront the implications of our quest for creative freedom, individual license, and autonomy" (268). Ultimately, both the Tall Convict and Harry Wilbourne do confront these implications, and they arrive at the same point of understanding, though Harry does so only after the effects of his nihilistic ideology have been fully manifested. From his prison cell, Harry comes to see what the Tall Convict has understood much earlier—that he must accept the circumstances that he has been cast into and the fact that he does not control his own fate ("it was not his life, he still and would ever be no more than the water bug upon the surface of the pond" [*Novels* 675]) but that, given this knowledge, he must still act as a responsible moral agent. Convicted of manslaughter, Harry is sentenced to "not less than fifty years" at Parchman, where he will join the Tall Convict in "hard labor" (*Novels* 713), at least for the two decades remaining on the latter's sentence. He will have ample time for reflection on the costs of his and Charlotte's quest.

For his part, as a result of his ordeal, the Tall Convict now has new subjects for contemplation. The convict's telling of his own story concludes with the suggestion that a deep well of memory of horrific and unspeakable events underlies his flat narrative, ending with the dynamiting of the Cajun's house. "That was all. But he remembered it, but quietly now" (*Novels* 831): in the not telling and in the suggestion of a depth of experience—a Marlow-like profundity that cannot be expressed in language—the authority of the convict's tale is underlined. Interestingly, the convict's remembering parallels the crucial motive for Harry's decision at the end of the novel for wanting to continue to live, even after receiving what amounts to a lifetime sentence. It certainly cannot be for any expectation of pleasure, nor for any hope of future success. Rather, he now realizes that "memory" can exist only within time and nature, the physical world in which he might have grasped his own immortality, not in the dry, deathly spaces that he and Charlotte have sought. Harry now joins the Tall Convict in the realization that consciousness resides only within the living "flesh" (*Novels* 715), a recognition that implies pity and love, the caring for and protecting of life.

In a profound observation, Edmond Volpe notes that "[t]he incapacity of language to recapture presence accounts for one of the primary aspects of the 'grief' which Harry accepts." His choice of "grief," Volpe points out, "indicates that while words form an irredeemably inadequate substitute for presence…the determination to endure even in light of this recognition, to continue using language because the alternative is oblivion, constitutes the affirmation of the creative artist" (86). Although Volpe finds that only Harry consciously faces this existential choice, this conception of the work of the creative artist seems to me little different from the Tall Convict's ideal of selfless responsibility in the face of almost universal chaos and destruction. In the end, both Harry and the Tall Convict have chosen "grief," and they will spend the rest of their lives, in or out of prison, reflecting on the meaning of their choice.

3

Faulkner's Requiem for the Past

Among other things, William Faulkner's major novels, from *The Sound and the Fury* to *Go Down, Moses*, represent a hard-won understanding of the author's relationship to the authority and traditional values of his culture. Within this canon, *If I Forget Thee, Jerusalem* contains Faulkner's most detailed and explicit consideration of his culture's conception of gender and of his own perspective on the subject. By contrast, Faulkner's later novels possess both greater assurance and an urgent instinct to sum up and conclude a long and troubled career. In its qualities of historical and moral reflection on a broad range of issues, *Requiem for a Nun* serves as exactly this sort of summation of Faulkner's entire canon. In its prose sections, the novel summarizes the relationship of the early settlers to the Native Americans, the rise and fall of plantation society, the epochal change brought about by the Civil War and Reconstruction, and the modernization of the South in the twentieth century, while in its dramatic scenes it relates Faulkner's concerns about the present and future to his lifelong contemplation of the southern past.

Requiem, however, is more than a précis of Faulknerian narrative interests because as a requiem—a mass conducted for the dead that invokes rest and peace—it implicitly advances a solution to the moral confusion and destructiveness that he has identified throughout his career. As Faulkner now understands, the damage of history can only be ameliorated by way of an unconditional commitment to principles that possess a grounding outside of history. In *Requiem*, perhaps for the first time in his career, Faulkner explicitly comments on the process by which historical contingency must be corrected, and this process relies on the power of a stable belief system to resist the force of change.

The very title of the novel identifies the work as an effort to find solace within a restless and unquiet mortal existence. In a backward gaze on the damage of modern history, and in reflection on his own role within this history, Faulkner seeks at the end of his writing career to come to terms with the central contradiction that had always existed within his depiction of southern history: an admiration for the heroic individualism of the founders and settlers in conflict with a painful awareness of diminishment and betrayal among their descendents. As an effort to make peace with his own history, the novel focuses very little on the issue of social justice and not at all on revenge; rather, it is a call for healing and forgiveness. After all, what justice can there really be after the bloodbath of slavery, war, and genocide that Faulkner has witnessed in the modern world? Still, the achievement of solace depends not on reparations but on making the effort to put things aright for the future, and the possibility of future justice depends on a careful scrutiny of the past and the present.

In Faulkner's view, modernization, by virtue of its inhuman organization of human life, its regimentation, and its conformity, threatens the idea of liberty upon which America was founded. The problem of the direction that modern America seems to be taking is one that Faulkner wrestles with again and again in *Requiem*, and the fact that he is so preoccupied with it reveals a new aspect of his art: an explicit concern with public and political issues. In Faulkner's political rhetoric one can see the effect of World War II on his sensibility: he now believes that his writing must serve a patriotic purpose, the equivalent to the experience of combat that was denied him in both world wars. If he was too young to serve in World War I and too old for the second, Faulkner could nonetheless serve his country honorably by adapting his imaginative powers to the needs of a modern democracy with all the economic, social, and psychological conflicts of his time.

Still, the prevailing conditions of regimentation and conformity are balanced and offset to some extent by the inherent goodness that Faulkner detects in the American people. Throughout *Jerusalem*, Faulkner stresses his belief in the providential history of America. The idea of American exceptionalism is worked into the novel as Faulkner describes America as a land of nearly endless opportunity. Despite the ravages of mankind on its environment and the repression of social injustice, America is a land where God has provided human beings with a special gift of abundance and a special destiny. It is important to note that Faulkner is utterly sincere in this assertion, and he may well be one of the last major authors in American literature to assert American exceptionalism without irony or qualification. There is nothing comparable in the works of Hemingway, Steinbeck, or in any of the major postwar authors with the possible exception of the late Saul Bellow.

Faulkner's *Requiem*, however, embodies not merely a traditional idea of providential history but a broader conservative ideology. Published in 1950, the play/novel is intercut with historical essays in which Faulkner not only recounts Mississippi history but interprets that history in the light of his own experience and that of his contemporaries. Thus, when he speaks of the Civil War, Faulkner describes the war as fought in the cause of states' rights, a conception of localism that guaranteed the right of states and by extension that of individuals to resist "federal meddling." It is important to unpack the web of meaning that Faulkner, like most southerners and westerners of his time (and of our own), attach to conceptions of local autonomy such as that projected in the idea of states' rights. Far from being the morally hollow catchphrase it appeared to be in the 1960s, discredited by the attempts to employ it in defense of state laws enforcing segregation, Faulkner's concept of states' rights refers to a fundamental principle of the Constitution: the constitutional protection reserving for the states all rights not specifically assigned to the federal government. This principle ensured local control, at the state level, of most functions of government, and it also ensured diversity of laws and cultures among the different states and regions. Furthermore, because of the assumption that a tighter cultural consensus would exist at the state level than at the federal, one might assume that the forms that government and law would take would be more perfectly suited to the local expectations of the people. As a result of local autonomy, the people would enjoy greater freedom from legal and bureaucratic control, and there would be less possibility of government devolving into tyranny. This, of course, was the principle not only of states' rights but of autonomous township councils, an idea that Thomas Jefferson, after leaving office, felt should have been inserted into the Constitution and whose absence was, as Jefferson saw it, a fateful mistake by the founders of American democracy.

In practice, southerners like Faulkner, through their insistence not only on states' rights but on liberty at the local and even at the individual level, were attempting to carry out Jefferson's plan of local councils and even to go beyond it. Yet the principle of local autonomy was hardly an invention of Jefferson or of the French Jacobin thinkers who influenced his writing: it is a basic principle of political philosophy reaching back from Jefferson to Locke, and from Locke to Aquinas to Aristotle. The idea that all but essential functions, notably that of national defense, be reserved for the states or local councils and that a wide range of individual liberties be protected is a foundational belief of Western political thought that has been repeated and restated countless times. It is a fundamental principle of Thomistic thought, for example, that agricultural land is best managed by individual or family ownership and that industrial production involve workers as co-owners or co-managers. The principle of local governance is the subject of Pope Pius XI's Encyclical *Quadragesimo Anno*: "It is an injustice, a grave evil and a disturbance of right order for a larger and higher organization to arrogate to itself functions which can be performed efficiently by smaller and lower bodies" (qtd. in Maritain, *Social and Political* 267). Thus, Faulkner's distrust of the expansion of federal powers, beginning with FDR and continuing in postwar administrations, is grounded in a tradition of local governance and individual freedom that can be traced to the very beginning of Western political thought.

In the context of American history, the perpetuation of a belief in local autonomy has been associated particularly with the experience of the frontier. From the early years of the Republic, marked by numerous rebellions against federal taxation and legal control, to the last years of the frontier, the westward movement carried with it a mythic ideal of independence and self-governance. As he describes the southern pioneers, Faulkner speaks of them in heroic terms as those who opened the wilderness to later settlement and so made possible the miracle of America itself. The record of frontier settlement was seriously marred, of course, by the fact of Native American disenfranchisement, but this problem is addressed and ingeniously dismissed via Faulkner's trope of settlers as "moccasin wearers" (*Requiem* 187). In speaking of those white men who not only disenfranchised the Indian but "had even stepped into the very footgear of them they dispossessed" (187), Faulkner's rhetoric implies not a disenfranchisement but a continuity between the Native Americans and the white settlers who admittedly have seized their lands but who have also adopted many of their ways. Enough of Indian culture has been passed down that the white settlers or at least some of them become the cultural descendents of Indians. In this figuration, America itself is thus the descendent of Native America. The Indian has never been disenfranchised; he has simply been reincarnated in the form of modern-day Americans.

Nonetheless, in contrast to this hopeful imagining of the continuity of Native American culture into the present, much of *Requiem for a Nun* suggests a counter-argument that the noble virtues of the past are as impermanent as everything else about American culture. Possibly the main difference between Americans and Europeans is just this fact; at some point in history European emigrants decided to leave their homeland and, having abandoned the old ways of their homeland to embark upon an uncertain new life, contributed to a different mentality among Americans. The European has lived not just for generations but "forever" or for as long as anyone can remember among the same people with a secure sense of identity and full knowledge of the home region. By contrast, Americans are forever moving and forever renewing their culture and their way of life. Always on the edge, they have never settled into a place and become "American." They really don't know what American means in the sense that someone from Scotland or Germany knows what it means to be Scottish or German. Americans have little sense of the permanent institutions or the rigid social hierarchies that Henry James portrayed in his works set in Europe. If anything, as James emphasized in *The American Scene*, America, especially in the decades of economic boom and mass immigration after the Civil War, was a place of socially turbulent and unpredictable forces bordering on the anarchic but affording energy and dynamism of a sort inconceivable in the Old World. In contrasting a cruder but vigorous America with a stagnant and corrupt Europe, James was giving voice to the crucial mythology of modern American democracy: America as the land of opportunity, America as the land of freedom and change.

The dilemma at the center of Faulkner's understanding of America is precisely this predicament of impermanence. The relocation of nearly every generation from its temporary "home," generally in the westward direction—from Europe to the East Coast of America, from the coast inland to the Piedmont, across the Appalachians to the Mississippi and then to the Pacific—involves a danger, a possible heedlessness and callousness, an uncritical enshrinement of cultural impermanence as the norm. An acceptance of rootlessness by an entire people carries with it all sorts of hazards including the inability to understand the intolerance of other peoples toward forms of risk and insecurity that are taken for granted within American society. Thus, the frontier experience has profound implications for the psychological, social, and political health of future generations of Americans long separated from the physical frontier, but these are difficulties that Faulkner largely ignores, for as his intricate prose sections make clear, the frontier is at the center of his thinking about America's legacy. Despite his ambivalence, the admission of potential harm that incessant movement and dislocation may cause, Faulkner ultimately embraces the frontier ethos as the dynamic and creative core of American character.

One characteristic of the frontier myth that Faulkner values above all is that of individualism. Everywhere in the prose sections of *Requiem*, as in the text of the play itself, Faulkner implies the dignity of the individual. The individual possesses the inalienable right to be treated as a person and identified as an individual, and to be allotted freedom of action within the circumstances that time and place have granted him as well as the required responsibilities. Even Nancy, despite her perfunctory treatment by the justice system, is accorded the dignity owed a human being. This is the point, perhaps, of Faulkner's characterization of her as a "nigger dope-fiend whore" (*Requiem* 109)—certainly the lowest social status that anyone in Faulkner's culture could imagine—and yet, when she finally speaks at her trial, Nancy is heard out. In fact, her words evoke a greater response than those of any speaker. Later, when Temple presents her case to the governor, it is accorded a hearing even though the dismissal of her appeal is a foregone conclusion. The point is that even Nancy falls within the ethos of individualism by which Faulkner's culture defines itself.

The primary purpose of the prose sections of *Requiem* is, in fact, to explore this ethos, a body of beliefs that Faulkner traces to the founding of the town of Jefferson and of Yoknapatawpha County and, beyond this, to the land's earliest settlers. As Faulkner traces a lineage from the founders to modern times, he shows that this cultural ethos continues even up to the period in which he is writing, even if it is threatened by various forces, including the homogenization of American culture and especially by the consequences of radical individualism itself. The main theme of the prose sections of the novel is exactly this problem of the survival of his own or of any cultural tradition in the face of a rationalistic modernity that, paradoxically, can be traced to the same origins of Reformation thought that are responsible for Faulkner's conception of individualism. Carried to an extreme, Luther's religion of faith evolves into an iconoclastic modernity of self-sovereignty and private ethics. The virtue of liberty that Faulkner celebrates can devolve into tyranny if it becomes blind to the necessary relationship of the individual to others and to those institutions and traditions that moderate and regulate this relationship and, most importantly, if it is overwhelmed by the consequences of radical individualism itself.

Faulkner's intention is not to write a philosophical treatise, but underlying his later writing is an instinctual grasp of the consequences of the Enlightenment pursuit of radical forms of selfhood and free will. The self-destructive contradictions within Enlightenment thought have been played out in the context of American culture, and perhaps nowhere is this more apparent than within the radically individualistic ethos of the frontier South. The Gothic elements of this culture so prominently featured in its literature are essentially the manifestations of a political and ethical philosophy that in its original and moderate form nurtured a dynamic awakening of industriousness and faith but that in its modern transmutation has come to seem radically inhuman. This transmutation is the very heart of Faulkner's interest in *Requiem*.

Everywhere Faulkner looks in this novel, in fact, he describes cultures that have turned away from their origins. As he traces this destructive transformation of cultures, Faulkner explores the psychic origins of the very process that gives rise to obsolescence, not merely the disappearance of a particular past—the Native American cultures, for example, displaced by the pioneers—but the continual and increasingly hectic series of obsolescences that transpire at an ever-more rapid pace, so that within a few generations the Indians are displaced by the early settlers, who are, in turn, displaced by the townspeople, who are then displaced by the post-Civil War boosters and carpetbaggers, who then are superceded by later generations. The modern period is not an exception to this cultural pattern but an acceleration of it, and we can see Faulkner's despair at the increasing pace of change during the post-World War II period.

The rebellion against one's inheritance is, of course, widespread if not universal within a culture that has historically located its very identity within the frontier experience. In fact, it may be that, to some extent, rebellion is a projection of the culture itself, a necessary adaptation within a modern world culture that will not permit stasis. In this sense, nearly everyone within Western culture is obliged to question his or her principles and to participate in a process of change that is itself the essential identity of Western culture since the Enlightenment, and yet it should be obvious that this process can take on a mind of its own and can give birth to a destructive process of cultural entropy to the point where self-questioning amounts to cultural paralysis. A wholesale rejection of all forms of tradition, all institutions and beliefs, results in what we see in Temple and Gowan: the alcoholism, hedonism, and self-contempt of a society demoralized by the fact that it has discarded its own past and its very sense of objectivity.

It seems likely, based on a reading of Faulkner's apprenticeship fiction and his early novels, that Faulkner himself participated in this rebellion to some extent. The tramp figure in his early *New Orleans Sketches*, along with the glamorously doomed pilots of the early stories and novels, are figures of enormous importance to our reading of Faulkner. They are self-destructive rebels, outside of society's norms and traditions. Joe Christmas and Thomas Sutpen are, of course, more mature products of this same Faulknerian strain of rebellion, as is Temple Drake. All of these are simply figures who, in the broad sense, represent an urgent need to question culture. Faulkner's letters also suggest that Faulkner himself entertained similar feelings, especially in the letters that he wrote to his mother. In fact, it is not going too far to say that Faulkner is Temple and that in the long meditation on Temple Drake, Faulkner is working out the consequences of his own rejection of Western culture.

The moment in her youth when Temple steps off the train with her date, Gowan Stevens, on the way to a football game: the image is crucial. She has been in motion, a frantic movement away from the traditional home in which she was reared; stepping off the train, she continues to be in motion, but now alone, she enters a new stage in which she will suffer the consequences of her rejection of tradition. She enters a world of self-definition and self-gratification, an utterly individualistic world of hedonism, impermanence, and anarchy. In this state, it is always the ruthless and violent who prevail, and so Popeye enters Temple's world as representative of the post-Christian modernity toward which she has been attracted all along. In this sense, Temple does not merely suffer the misfortune of wandering into the cold, cruel world of the gangster: she enters it by way of her own desire. After the period in the Memphis brothel, Temple is carried back to her patriarchal home but in terms of her spiritual life, she does not come to any resolution in her relationship to her inherited culture until that resolution is forced upon her by Nancy Mannigoe's act of sacrificing one of Temple's children. It is at this point that Temple is able to reflect on the pattern that her life as a whole has taken: her youthful rebellion, the destructive consequences, the cynicism and demoralization that follow, her nihilistic period of spiritual death just before the loss of her child. This crisis and the reflection that accompanies it lead to a sweeping reversal in Temple's perspective, and one might well explore the period of incubation and composition of *Requiem* from the early 1930s to the late 1940s in order to know whether Faulkner himself underwent this sort of spiritual crisis.

What is lost within a culture of radical skepticism is not merely what Faulkner sometimes referred to as the values of the "old people," the Native American culture that he so much admires and that of the whites who learned from them, but the influence of *any* sort of viable historical tradition. It is one thing for the European settlers to displace an earlier native culture; it is another to disavow the validity of any tradition, including one's own, and this is the problem that Faulkner addresses in the dramatic scenes of the book. Temple and Gowan's problem lies in human nature itself: the insatiable drive toward extremes that is present in all peoples but most apparent in those who are heir to the frontier ethos of constant change. Perhaps because of this legacy, Temple and Gowan have lost their grip on the past; they have no ethical bearing in their lives because they do not view their lives in relation to any historical or ethical tradition.

The ending of the dramatic section, in which Nancy urges Temple simply to "believe," is a powerful statement of Faulkner's solution to this problem, but it also seems an implicit admission of despair at ever finding within his culture a consensus of common beliefs that would function as an alternative to sheer individual will—the injunction simply to keep the faith no matter what. The word "believe" sums up what is missing in Temple's and Gowan's lives, but Nancy offers no clue of what to believe in or of how to regain this belief. Clearly, what is involved is an opposition to the destructive force of change that Faulkner sees in all periods of American culture but most markedly in the twentieth century. As Leszek Kolakowski shows in "The Revenge of the Sacred in Secular Culture," the impact of belief in the sacred is inherently conservative: throughout human civilization, religious belief has "reaffirmed and stabilized the structure of society" (70). It is not merely that religion was employed to buttress conservative institutions that govern civil society; it is, as Kolakowski explains, that belief in a sacred order of existence is inextricably tied to our ability to perceive fundamental moral distinctions: even those most obvious distinctions "between war and peace, sovereignty and servitude, invasion and liberation, equality and despotism" (70) are lost in the absence of a ground of faith.

As Nancy employs the idea, of course, belief does not suggest particular religious dogma of any kind but the capacity for belief in the binding power of tradition itself: in other words, an act of reflection that amounts to a slowing of the pace of change, even to the point of stepping outside the process of change and of conceiving one's life within a stable tradition of ethical distinctions. Still, the problem is that one's very ability to express a consciousness of the lapse of traditional belief attests a process of decline in belief that is already complete or nearly complete, and it is not enough simply to encourage the reinstatement of tradition. The very ability to conceptualize the "problem of faith" implies that one is standing outside of a belief system that one would otherwise not be able to imagine as problematic. The prompting to "believe" at the end of *Requiem* strikes a weak note because at the point at which it is necessary to persuade others to believe, belief must already be in doubt. Faulkner imagines Temple and Gowan as leading their family back to earlier traditions of their culture or perhaps adapting these traditions to the present in some way, but it is the capacity to believe in tradition of any kind—the tacitly acknowledged belief that contains in its very existence the capacity to arrest the destructive movement of history—that is most in doubt. The tension between obsolescence and belief is hardly relieved by Faulkner's emphasis upon the problematic nature of faith in the context of modern skepticism.

On the other hand, there is no doubt as to what motivates the frantic changes that Faulkner sees taking place in Jefferson: it is the power of unbridled capitalism, an element that existed from the earliest days of settlement but that has now become vastly accelerated and seems to have taken on a life of its own. Planters like Sutpen, even as they were engaged in a ruthless exploitation of man and nature, are still individualists who, while they cannot control their unbridled dreams, can nonetheless be admired for their courage, but the developers represented by Redmond who arrive after the Civil War are a class of men of a different and more insidious type: these capitalists do not so much fail in controlling their appetites as, like Flem Snopes, they possess no real appetites since they are really controlled by their bloodless pursuit of money for its own sake. Because of the alienating power of capital, the pace of social change becomes more and more inflexible, frenetic, and even mad to the point where the courthouse gang—the parasitic local politicians who occupy the lucrative county offices—attempts to raze the courthouse itself every four years in order to obtain the grants of federal money that will line their own pockets. What Faulkner sees, in sum, is now no longer a society of strong individualists, men who are to be admired even though many of them lead tragic and even amoral lives, but smaller and smaller types, utterly controlled by the deterministic forces of economics.

Faulkner also understands the connection between the increasing force of capitalism and the centralization of government. Like President Eisenhower, who attempted to defeat the growing power of federal bureaucracies during the 1950s, especially that of the Pentagon, Faulkner recognized the danger to democracy posed by the centralization of vast resources within governmental departments. With the new infusion of federal funds that began during the administration of FDR in the 1930s, the parasitic class that relied on government jobs was multiplied manyfold. At the same time, not only individuals but towns, counties, and even states were losing their sense of autonomy as they became dependent on the federal government. Since decisions were no longer made at the local level—as in Faulkner's view, they should have been—the national culture became more and more homogenized. The resulting loss of local cultural diversity resulted in a dangerous unanimity of national opinion, one that could lead the nation into destructive actions that might otherwise be moderated by debate or stalled by resistance. In Faulkner's eyes, the emergence of a single national culture dominated by an uncritical consensus was a monstrous consequence of federal power.

In all of this, there is the voice of the social and fiscal conservative's suspicion of federal bureaucracy that would later become an even more prominent aspect of southern politics. Faulkner understands that federal funding is creating a dependent client class and that, in a vicious cycle, this class will support greater federal funding that, in turn, will only increase the numbers of the client class until, eventually, the federal government controls the entire economy. The result will be a government that is not accountable to the people, and as the people become more and more dependent and less entrepreneurial, they will become both impoverished and demoralized. The intention of the welfare state, after all, is not to enrich the public at large but to ensure that no one class is better off than any other; it does not aim to create wealth but to impose an equality of scarcity. Needless to say, this political development was utterly abhorrent to Faulkner's way of thinking.

On the whole, Faulkner's portrait of postwar America is thus a frightening scenario of declining values, spread of government influence, and failure of individual responsibility, yet, if the march of progress seems unstoppable, Faulkner provides some hope. While the generation of what he calls the "irreconcilables"(those unreconstructed southerners with a firm sense of continuity with the past) seemed to be dying off at the turn of the century, surprisingly their number had increased substantially by mid-century, and Faulkner suggests that an increasing number of irreconcilables will appear in the future. Some of these are the children of "outlanders" who have moved to Mississippi from other regions of the country and who have "become" Yoknapatawphians—that is, they have acquired an interest in the legendry of the town and county where they now live, even though their families have only arrived within the past one or two generations.

Perhaps an even stronger source of hope lies in what is represented by Cecelia Farmer's scratching of her name and date onto the jail window. Faulkner writes that this voice is "invincible." It speaks across the decades of the old times before the Civil War, and the power of this voice, which expresses itself in the etching of a name on a piece of glass, is enough to hold the attention of the casual visitor to the jail and make that visitor wish to hear her story from the past. Still, when Cecelia Farmer scratches her name on the pane of glass in the jail and dates it April 16, 1861, several ironies attend this action, not least of which is the fact that her father, the jailor, is a failed farmer named "Farmer"; the fact that Cecelia herself is too frail and anemic to help with any of the household chores but spends her days musing is another. As the embodiment of a popular cultural mythology—the southern belle awaiting the return of her promised love—Cecelia is lacking in nearly every respect, and in this sense she resembles Temple and more obliquely Nancy, each of whom seems to have failed in the role expected of her, yet all three women are alike in the crucial sense of possessing an inexhaustible voice or will. In her calm patience and in her simple constancy, the essential fact of her remaining in Jefferson to await the return of her love and in what follows, her patient durability as a married woman and matriarch, Cecelia does live up to the requirements of her social role, but she does something more. It is not merely in playing a role but in the instinctual persistence of the life force within her that Cecelia becomes a heroic and even a spiritual paragon. In effect, she embodies the human drive toward achievement, survival, even immortality, and, particularly in light of her own glaring lack of qualifications, Cecelia appears to suggest that this divine instinct exists within all human beings, even in Temple and Nancy.

In the prose sections of *Requiem*, the figure of Cecelia Farmer offers a hopeful opposition to the force of progress and change: in effect, she creates her own immortality by stopping time. Similarly, in the dramatic sections of the novel, Nancy Mannigoe, speaking "inappropriately" (as the courtroom audience believes) as she cries out "Yes, Lord," has the power to block the unthinking and inhuman movement of the trial. Her voice intercedes and breaks the routine of what is expected. In the same way, Nancy's call on Temple to "believe" is a force, like that of Cecelia Farmer, that is set against the reflexive movement in which Temple and everyone else in the play is caught up.

Requiem for a Nun is Faulkner's meditation on mortality, in its own way not unlike Plato's *Symposium* or Shakespeare's *The Tempest*. What Faulkner attempts in *Requiem* is a form of achievement in the classical sense as an artist who puts his work into the public realm for the admiration of readers, a form of artistic creation that carries with it a distinctly ethical premise concerning not only the role of the artist within society but also the relation of society to enduring patterns of cultural meaning. As Hannah Arendt points out in *The Human Condition*, as both the private and public realms in the modern world are subsumed into "society," this form of achievement is increasingly viewed with skepticism: in Hobbes' terms as "vainglory" or in the terms of Adam Smith as merely an attempt to produce "cultural capital." Faulkner's impulse to preserve a classical conception of the artist as one engaged in a competition of the greatest importance and as one who receives the laurel wreath for achievement is out of place in the modern age. Faulkner is well aware of this fact, and, in this sense, *Requiem* is an assertion of an impossible dream; it is finally an elegy for the artist conceived of in the classical sense and at the same time a dirge for modern man. Ultimately, Faulkner presents no solution other than an attempt to return to a more traditional conception of the artist's public role. At the same time, however, his writing affords a more realistic attestation of the growing power of socialization.

What Faulkner perceives in the course of his meditation on mortality is a corruptible and fleeting world around him, a place in which physical objects become obsolescent nearly as soon as they are created and in which human lives are rendered meaningless by the way in which accomplishment, however great, is undermined and cancelled out by the flow of time. In this world, decay and destruction prevail, and whatever human beings create is subject to the devastating force of change, yet in this transient place, men and women everywhere are still driven by their dream of immortality. This was the dream of the founders of Jefferson, as it was of America's founders. It is the point of the "irrevocable design" of the Frenchman who fashions the courthouse and lays out the plan of the larger town of Jefferson. It is, of course, also the dream of others who are less successful, including the architect's master, Thomas Sutpen, as well as his contemporaries, Alec Holston, Thomas Jefferson Pettigrew, Compson, Ratcliffe, and all of the others who view themselves as founders. This generation, after all, dies off within a few years of the moment when the town is officially founded, and the founding itself seems, from our perspective, a pathetically inadequate gesture, consisting as it does of the erection of a temporary courthouse that is nothing more than a second-room addition to the existing jail.

The impermanence of life is also the central subject of the dramatic sections of the book devoted to Temple Drake Stevens and Nancy Mannigoe. Intercut with the historical prose sections of the novel, Faulkner's stage drama connects society's past with the immediate present. After all, Nancy is facing the most blatant challenge to life, the death sentence that will be carried out within a few days, and Temple, whose misery seems to mirror the condition of her black house servant, faces what amounts to her own lifetime sentence of remorse. As she says, "tomorrow and tomorrow and tomorrow" her guilt will continue for the part she played in the failure of her marriage and for her responsibility in the death of her child, albeit at Nancy's hand, and for Nancy's own death.

In the final analysis, *Requiem* reads like a dirge devoted to the decline of freedom in America, a decline that finds its paradoxical origin in its own excesses and the destruction of all civilization, and yet this dirge ends with the triumph of Nancy's faith even in the face of certain death. The contrapuntal elements within this complex novel can be traced to the contradictions that Faulkner identifies within American ideology itself: the empowering force of religious faith over against the destructiveness of blind faith in one's own cultural ethos; the justifiable celebration of human liberty versus the moral failure of radical individualism; the success of entrepreneurial capitalism in conflict with the offensive abuses of unbridled capitalism. The effect of these contradictions is a predictable cynicism in regard to the possibility of any sort of belief, and it is precisely this reaction that is evident in Temple, but Nancy's belief in immortality and in the possibility of belief itself is a further and perhaps unexpected turn in the narrative. It comprises a reaction against Temple's rebellion and an attempt to save Temple and, in fact, her entire civilization by reversing the cynical and demoralized rejection of faith that has become the norm among so-called educated Americans in the modern period. Nancy's apparently simplistic teaching, it turns out, is a response informed by a complex understanding of Temple's spiritual situation. It is also effective, for in the end Temple joins Nancy in an act of faith signaled by her reuniting with her husband and rejoining a productive family life. The true nature of immortality lies in something more profound than human enterprise, will, or even creativity: it can be located within the ability to believe, even in the face of certain defeat.

This call for belief is Faulkner's response to the increasing pace of social change within American culture. It is a reaction to the decline of American culture into a condition of cynicism and demoralization that is itself a response to the excesses that have accompanied the triumphant expansion of American culture from its founding to the present. By combining the dramatic sections of the novel with the prose passages, Faulkner allows us to locate our cynical rebellion against Western culture within the historical context of a dynamic, enormously productive, but ruthless history. One hopes that, with the insight that this complex novel affords, we will understand that our own existence need not comprise simply another obsolescent stage in an ever more reductive historical process. Like Cecelia Farmer's mark on the glass, our culture can choose to abide in ways that are more productive than merely surrendering to our own sense of malaise, and like Nancy Mannigoe's call for belief, we can oppose the inhuman forces of change and discover our place within a binding order of faith and tradition.

4

Fitzgerald's "Dream of the South"

As F. Scott Fitzgerald tells us in an arresting metaphor, "poetry is a Northern man's dream of the South" (*Bodley Head* 5: 484). In this complex trope from "The Last of the Belles," Fitzgerald suggests both the luxuriant beauty of the South and its illusory quality. Written from the point of view of a narrator who is looking back on his failed love affair with a southern belle—"the lost midsummer world of my early twenties" (*Bodley Head* 5: 484)—the metaphor conveys an aching sense of nostalgia for vanished youth and of disillusionment with the hopes of youth as well. As Fitzgerald's narrator remembers them, the Georgia nights of his youth possessed an almost mystical quality of "brightness" and warmth, but for this very reason the loss of Ailie Calhoun, the eponymous last belle, strikes Andy as representing the end of all hope for himself and his generation. Lacking the "brightness" that Ailie and her world supplied, the narrator is driven back into the northern world of unfeeling darkness. In the summer before departing for World War I, Andy tells us, "the South sang to us" (*Bodley Head* 5: 481), yet recounting his lost dreams, Andy is filled with an enormous sense of disillusionment.

Fitzgerald's dream of the South is an escape from what he has come to see as the selfish individualism and materialism of the North. In contrast to the life of business and conspicuous consumption that dominates the North, Fitzgerald views the agrarian South in the same way that many of his contemporaries did: as an escape from the pressures of modern society. Not yet having arrived at the destructive stage of alienation that characterizes the North, the South is not only a potential site of escape, it is also a model of what the North might be. Unfortunately, like all dreams, Fitzgerald's southern dream is insubstantial and, in time, gives way to the reality that the South is essentially no different from the North. In his later reflections, Fitzgerald comes to see that southerners can be entirely as selfish and materialistic as northerners, and perhaps they are worse because of their hypocritical assertion that the South remains a land of grace and manners even as it develops along the lines of the North.

To understand how Fitzgerald's dream of the South was formed, one needs to examine the popular media of his day, especially the stories and feature articles about the South in mass-circulation magazines such as *The Saturday Evening Post*. In addition, Fitzgerald was undoubtedly aware of newspaper accounts of natural disasters in the South, notably the coverage of the Mississippi flood of 1927; of popular radio venues, such as Will Rogers' nationally syndicated weekly program; and of innumerable filmed and staged dramas, from *The Birth of a Nation* (1915) to *The Story of Temple Drake* (1933), based on William Faulkner's novel, *Sanctuary*. Of course, there was much in the popular treatment of the South in which he showed no interest: stories of mountaineers, southern folklore, poor whites, and racial humor. Fitzgerald, we shall see, was highly selective in what he drew from the popular media and skillful in the subtle adaptation of this material for his own purposes. To a remarkable degree, he focused on the South's genteel impoverishment, its cultural provinciality, and its vulnerability, especially the fragile sexuality of its young women. Fitzgerald was much interested in stories of romantic encounters between southern and non-southern characters, a motif that Ida Jeter connects with the contemporary mood of national reconciliation based on "a shared national sympathy and respect for the humiliated region and white supremacy" (33).

During Fitzgerald's most productive years as a writer, the early 1920s to the mid-1930s, certain images and themes recur in the popular depiction of the South, and to a large extent these images and themes reflect the national culture's long-standing conception of the South in light of its defeat in the Civil War. In this portrayal, the South was both idealized and dismissed: admired for its heroic survival (for instance, the resourcefulness of its spinsters managing to survive on nothing after the Civil War and the ambitiousness of *some* of its young men, especially those who flee the South to pursue their dreams of success in the northern cities) yet, at the same time, regarded as weak and backward; much loved as the "magnolia and moonlight" South with its aristocracy, graceful living, and elegant manners yet represented as decadent, a seductive but ultimately destructive site of corruption replete with moonshine liquor, gambling, and seemingly innate sexual depravity.[1]

Accompanying these images of southernness one might expect to find a significant treatment of race. No matter how difficult the racial problems in the North might be, the obvious fact was that the legacies of slavery—Jim Crow segregation, political suppression, and lynching—were, in some sense, distinctively southern. As if by some gentleman's agreement, however, this fundamental social difference between the North and the South was largely elided in the popular media, in which lynching, for example, was rarely fictionalized. In place of a realistic critique of race, writers such as Octavius Cohen capitalized on the appeal of racial humor at the expense of African Americans. As we shall see, the mood of regional reconciliation and the requisite silencing of racial concern that accompanied it would become a central element in Fitzgerald's adaptation of the popular image of the South. Not that racial issues formed a large part of his depiction of the South: his main focus was on the process of reconciliation itself and what this homogenizing of regional cultures within the nation would mean for the South and for the nation as a whole.

The 1920s saw expanding horizons for most Americans outside the South, and stories and articles in the national media were increasingly aimed at an audience that was, or aspired to be, middle class. This writing depicted the South as the nation's poor cousin, at best the locale of Florida winter resorts or of Georgia golf courses. *Post* stories such as Joseph Hergesheimer's "Captive Pass" (1 May 1926), in which a local Florida man serves as a guide for wealthy northern tourists, or Thomas McMorrow's "To Let, on Flagler Street" (6 February 1926) are typical. Numerous Florida stories by Marjory Stoneman Douglas report on the activities of snowbirds, real estate agents, cruise ship employees, and charter boat operators. In "Jacob's Ladder," published on 20 August 1927, Fitzgerald employs one of the more common characters of *Post* fiction: the Florida real estate millionaire. After developing laryngitis that threatens his musical career, Jacob Booth "bought a plantation in Florida and spent five years turning it into a golf course," Fitzgerald writes. "When the land boom came in 1924 he sold his real estate of eight hundred thousand dollars" (*Bodley Head* 5: 162).

Money, and the prestige and power that accompany it, are crucial elements in most fictional accounts of the South in the 1920s. Stories that feature a northern banker and an impoverished southern maiden are so numerous as to form an important sub-genre. Overwhelmingly, the South functions, by way of the absence of prosperity and modernity, as a gauge of northern progress. If we accept the image of the South in the popular magazines, the region was populated almost exclusively by hapless bumpkins, illiterate hillbillies, impoverished spinsters, and smiling, subservient blacks—along with a sizable population of good ol' boys that Fitzgerald referred to as "jelly beans." The title of Charles Wertenbaker's "Will You Walk a Little Faster?" (*Saturday Evening Post* 20 October 1928), the story of a Virginia father who attempts to prod his lazy son into success, reveals much about the nation's doubts concerning southern initiative.

Fitzgerald adapted this stereotype of the lazy southerner in several stories. More often than not, Fitzgerald adhered to the accepted wisdom that the South was a region of stagnation and idleness. For young women growing up in the South, the apparent lack of ambition in southern men raised doubts concerning their marriagability. As a result, in the popular imagination they were often paired with northerners whose prospects seemed better. In the way they were depicted, their economic dependency coupled with their proverbial "charm" and beauty made them especially appealing to men from outside the South. This relationship was, of course, a crucial element in Fitzgerald's personal life as it was in his fiction, but it was a transaction that would have seemed natural enough, given its frequency in the popular imagination of the time. In "Big Time" by William McNutt, for instance, a woman named Chery Wallace from New Orleans refuses to marry a southern newspaperman because of his impoverishment (*Saturday Evening Post* 29 May 1929). Similarly, in Joseph Hergesheimer's *Post* story, "Love in the United States" (7 September 1929), an elderly New Yorker returns to a southern city, carrying his most valuable possession: the photograph of the seventeen-year-old sweetheart of his youth.

Another familiar stereotype concerning the South was the idea that climate shapes character: the southern heat is responsible for an ingrained laziness, slowness, and lack of ambition. As Fitzgerald wrote in "The Jelly-Bean" (1920): "In this heat nothing mattered. All life was weather, a waiting through the hot where events had no significance for the cool that was soft and caressing like a woman's hand on a tired forehead. Down in Georgia there is a feeling—perhaps inarticulate—that this is the greatest wisdom of the South…" (*Bodley Head* 5: 218–19). Of course, the very label "jelly-bean," reserved for young southern males, is broadly dismissive. Fitzgerald was never so derisive as when he described Jim Powell, the protagonist of "The Jelly-Bean," as one who "grew lazily all during Jelly-bean season, which is every season, down in the land of the Jelly-beans well below the Mason-Dixon line" (*Bodley Head* 5: 198).

In another story, "The Swimmers," he cleverly deploys the image of the Virginia aristocrat, which in the popular imagination was another thing entirely than the "jelly-bean," in defense of one aspect of his "dream" of the South: the conviction that, while most southerners are either demented jelly-beans, incapable of any sort of accomplishment, or New South-style boosters who, like many Americans, mistake monetary success for social standing, there remains in the South a small class of true gentlemen possessed of wealth and graced with manners. This figure, which may have been suggested both by its common appearance in popular magazine fiction and also by Fitzgerald's own ancestry, involved Fitzgerald in artistic difficulties and, as Ruth Prigozy contends, must be judged as flawed and "mechanical" in its design (121). Nonetheless, in his departure from the conventional figure of the *impoverished* aristocrat,[2] Fitzgerald attempted something original. Published in the *Post* on 19 October 1929, "The Swimmers" describes Henry Clay Marston, who, after marrying a fickle French wife, Choupette, returns to his hometown of Richmond with his family. Marston is a stereotype of the proud southern aristocrat: "a Virginian of the kind who are prouder of being Virginians than of being Americans" (*Bodley Head* 5: 191), the sort of man for whom dueling still seems an attractive solution to his wife's affair with Charles Wiese. At the end of the story, having divorced Choupette and gained custody of their children in order to protect them from an immoral upbringing at the hands of Choupette and Wiese, Marston returns to Europe, coincidentally on the same ship as the unnamed Virginia girl whom he had rescued four years previously in France. In this positive treatment of the southern aristocrat, Fitzgerald created a figure not unlike that used by Margaret Mitchell seven years later in the character of Ashley Wilkes, except that Marston seems more competent and effectual.

Fitzgerald's portrayal of the southern belle involved more complexity than did his depiction of southern men.[3] In "The Popular Girl," Fitzgerald writes of Yanci Bowman and her father, residents of a midwestern city but descendants of an aristocratic southern family. As Mrs. Rogers tells Scott Kimberly, Yanci's "grandfather was a senator or governor or something in one of the Southern States [apparently Maryland]" (*Bodley Head* 5: 17). As in *The Great Gatsby*, the distinction between Yanci's midwestern and southern traits is elided: "She adored New York with a great impersonal affection—adored it as only a Middle Western or Southern girl can" (24). As a "Middle Western or Southern girl," Yanci is drawn to the activity, the glamour, and the wealth of New York and to its status as the nation's "center." Fashionable, influential, and dominant, it is everything that the provincial regions of the Middle West and the South are not. Despite her impoverishment following the death of her spendthrift father, and following a comedy of miscalculations, Yanci presumably finds a place for herself in the East, with her future marriage to Scott. Yanci is the impoverished provincial girl who, by virtue of her charm and beauty (and her vulnerability), is attractive to the wealthy young Easterner, Scott Kimberly ("an orphan with half a million of his own" [18]). (By contrast, marriages within the provincial regions are "marriages of environment, of resignation, or even of boredom" [17].) While the story clearly conveys that Yanci and Scott are an "ideal couple," this pairing raises questions concerning the reasons for the match, and especially for the regional element in Yanci's appeal. It is an appeal that Scott feels immediately upon seeing her on the dance floor: "She was the incarnation of all in which the dance failed—graceful youth, arrogant, languid freshness and beauty that was sad and perishable as a memory in a dream" (17). That dream-like but vulnerable freshness and beauty, suggesting that Yanci's charm is to a large extent the creation of the viewer, is a quality that Fitzgerald singles out in all figures of the southern belle, and since the charm is dream-like, it is inevitably transient and insubstantial.

In "The South of the Mind: The Changing Myth of the Lost Cause in the Life and Work of F. Scott Fitzgerald," P. Keith Gammons offers a valuable discussion of the treatment of the southern belle figure in Fitzgerald's fiction. Gammons suggests that Fitzgerald's fascination with the fictional southern belle, and perhaps with Zelda Sayre in real life, was related to a conflict in his mind between the appeal of the Lost Cause—a mythologizing of the Old South related to the southern beliefs of his father, Edward Fitzgerald—and his growing sense during the 1920s of the corruption of the American Dream in relation to those very ideals of honor and courtesy represented by the Old South. In Gammons' reading, the southern belle plays a central role in Fitzgerald's imagination as the embodiment of the southern ideal, although he "never gave any practical credence to the very real hope of the southerner for eventual cultural, if not political, restoration" (107). In this reading, Fitzgerald's early story, "The Ice Palace" (1920), reflects the first stage, a point at which Fitzgerald gave credence to the southern myth. As early as 1922, however, in his comments to Edmund Wilson concerning Zelda's "complete, and full-hearted selfishness and chill-mindedness" (qtd. in Gammons 108), Fitzgerald's belief in the southern belle and in the myth of the Old South had been shattered, and in later portrayals of the belle—Daisy Buchanan in *The Great Gatsby* (1924) and Ailie Calhoun in "The Last of the Belles" (1929)—Fitzgerald's treatment of the southern myth was bitterly ironic. In Gammons' view, Fitzgerald's rejection of the southern myth coincided with his disillusionment with the American Dream and the failure of his belief in the continuation of the virtues of the American frontier. "[T]he death of both the southern and the American dream" is shown in the portrait of Daisy in *The Great Gatsby*. Indeed, the southern belle—once held up as a potential model of beauty and cultivation—is now imagined as "degenerative" (Gammons 110).

Gammons' analysis addresses the crux of the problem in interpreting Fitzgerald's belle figures: the fact that the belle is capable of transformation from the alluring dream of charm and grace to the harsh reality of selfish opportunism. Gammons' reading is, thus, extremely valuable in the way that it focuses on the crucial fact of the "two Souths" that existed in Fitzgerald's thinking: the favored Old South, an exotic land of sweetness and light, and the despised New South, which aspired to rejoin the North in its mercantile calling. It is important, of course, to note that Fitzgerald's disillusionment with the South was not the direct product of his relationship with the real-life belle, Zelda Sayre, and that, in fact, his recognition of the insubstantiality of the dream predated *The Great Gatsby* and "The Last of the Belles" by several years. The problem that "The Jelly-Bean" raises is that in 1920—at the same time that he wrote "The Ice Palace" and before his marriage to Zelda—Fitzgerald was already capable of an utterly damning treatment of the southern mythology. A reading of "The Jelly-Bean" should cause us to realize that Fitzgerald's attitudes toward the southern subject were even more conflicted than Gammons and others suggest, and this *before* his marriage to Zelda and contemporaneous with "The Ice Palace."

Long before he met Zelda, Fitzgerald's image of the belle had been shaped by such popular figures as the actress Ruth Draper and the fictional characters in the novel *Marse Chan*, but these conventional notions were then complicated by his skeptical temperament. The belle type is sweet—overly sweet—and charming, deceptively so. She is at once gracious and selfish, childlike and insincere, spoiled, pampered, flirtatious, and, of course, irresistible. It is not necessary to conceive of Fitzgerald's disillusionment with the belle as the outcome of Zelda's fall from grace: in the general culture, the belle had always been seen as insincere and treacherous. Indeed, part of her allure, as Margaret Mitchell understood in the creation of Scarlett O'Hara, was her potential as a femme fatale. While Fitzgerald only hints at the fact, it is probable that the southern belle was also enchanting because of her vulnerability, a vulnerability that is the product of her region's economic disempowerment. Andy, the narrator of "The Last of the Belles," says that he "had grown to love Tarleton" (*Bodley Head* 5: 474), and what he loves is, essentially, its frailty, its weakness, its position of dependence in relation to his own culture. Ailie Calhoun, heroine of "The Last of the Belles" is precisely this sort of irresistible but destructive figure. She "causes" the death of Horace Canby, who crashes his plane out of despair at the prospect of her engagement to his rival, Bill Knowles, who has just returned from training in Texas to ask for her hand. As with all of Fitzgerald's belles, Ailie seems essentially insincere and manipulative, yet she is a fascinating woman that the northern soldiers find irresistible. Even her insincerity is enchanting, hinting at an underlying corruption that, in the context of the Jazz Age rebellion against puritan values, was by no means unappealing.

At the end of "The Last of the Belles," Andy washes his hands of the South. As he says, following his visit to Ailie six years after officer training school, after finding that Ailie will marry a man from Savannah, "the South would be empty for me forever" (*Bodley Head* 5: 488). It is an interesting metaphor: if the South was "full" before, in what sense was it "full"? Why is it now "empty"? Is it more than the conventional lover's lament of lost love and the emptiness of life? In his reading of "The Last of the Belles," Gammons offers a convincing answer. Gammons finds that Fitzgerald, now disillusioned with the southern belle, connects the belle with the New South as well as the Old so that the conventional southern belle is now seen as an illusion. "In its place," Gammons writes, "he saw a vessel of deceit, hiding a New South savagery behind the beautiful facade" (111).[4]

In southern history, the New South was the beginning of a period of industrialization and urbanization that would lift southern people out of their low-wage economy and that would, eventually, end the regional economic imbalance that resulted from the Civil War and Reconstruction. In social and economic terms, the New South was a return to a more equitable relationship among regional economies in the United States, and it was largely through a process of industrialization and commercial enterprise that progressive social development in the South, including advances in education, health, and racial cooperation, was enabled. Fitzgerald, who had once embraced the Old South myth, found the developing region "empty," and this emptiness was connected with the modernization that Fitzgerald saw taking place in the South. Because its economic development led the South toward the same spiritual desolation that Fitzgerald imagined for the industrial landscape of the North, the New South was figured as barren. Paradoxically, in "The Last of the Belles," for Ailie to marry a northerner and leave the South would have proven her region's incapacity and thus its "virtue" as a "full" locus ("filled" with frailty, dependence, loss); for her to marry a Southerner, as she now plans to do, leaves the South "empty" for Andy, since it proves the region's ability to retain her (rather than full, the southern topos is now "empty," that is, economically strong, "lacking" dependence, not focused on the mythology of defeat). As a progressive New South, it no longer satisfies the national culture's need for a fantasized alternative to modernity. It is no longer mysteriously "other," but merely one of us, another New Jersey.

The harsh portrayal of both southern men and southern women suggests that the impetus behind Fitzgerald's southern stories was not only the deteriorating relationship with Zelda but his interest in pursuing a cultural critique of the South based on quite outdated assumptions concerning the South's place within the national culture and economy. Fitzgerald's conception leaves the South in a double bind: lacking the commercial impetus of the North, southerners appear as lazy, unambitious, and inept (the jelly-bean); embracing modernization, they become grotesque travesties of the progressive mission.

The jelly-bean was by far the more common stereotype, and in his stories aimed at mass-circulation publications, Fitzgerald focused on this image. In this reading, southerners are simply not capable of making the leap from the small-minded, puritanical culture of the rural South to the modern, progressive cities of the North. As in the *Post* story "Valhalla-Bound" by Chester T. Crowell (4 September 1926), which exposes the unpleasantness of the southern small town, the popular image focused on the provinciality of southern society. In an age in which Americans measured the importance of their cities by the height of their skyscrapers, the traditionally agrarian South had little to offer. In "The Dance," published in *Red Book Magazine* (June 1926), Fitzgerald writes of the narrator's "rather curious horror of small towns" (*Bits of Paradise* 140), especially of southern small towns. In such places, Fitzgerald claims, "the men and the girls speak a language wherein courtesy is combined with violence, fanatic morality with corn-drinking recklessness, in a fashion which I can't understand. In 'Huckleberry Finn' Mark Twain described some of those towns perched along the Mississippi River, with their fierce feuds and their equally fierce revivals—and some of them haven't fundamentally changed beneath their new surface of flivvers and radios. They are deeply uncivilized to this day" (*Bits of Paradise* 141).

In the course of the story, Fitzgerald presents a cast of southern grotesques that rivals Twain's. The Saturday night before she is to leave Davis (the fictional name for a small southern city of 25,000), the narrator attends a dance at the country club in the company of Charley Kincaid, his fiancée Marie Bannerman, Joe Cable, and Catherine Jones. Fitzgerald's characterization of the group is highly stereotyped: Joe Cable is "the son of a former governor, a handsome, dissipated and yet somehow charming young man," while Marie Bannerman, with her heavily rouged cheeks and powdered nose and chin, her unfashionable clothes, her "shining black" hair, her "half-closed" eye (*Bits of Paradise* 142) and, as we later observe, her flirtatious infidelity, is the picture of provincial bad taste and weakness of character. While the young couples dine and dance at the country club, a Negro is being hunted in the swamp outside town. The fact that he will certainly be lynched is casually ignored by the southerners even if it troubles the narrator for a moment. Southern youths stand around the dance floor, "almost all of them cheerful with corn-liquor" (*Bits of Paradise* 146). The narrator finds Catherine Jones' "barbaric" dance—an early rendition of the Charleston—particularly offensive. As one of the few young women who drinks liquor, Catherine seems to embody the hypocrisy of a region that pretends to "manners" and aristocracy but that is given over to decadent self-indulgence. Like the southern climate and landscape (all too often swampy and overgrown), southern society seems to betray an instinctual sensuality and grossness. It is this aspect of society, especially among southern women, that is suggested by Catherine's dance: a dance that is based on "Negro" rhythms and motions, and that goes along with Catherine's drinking and the lushness and barely disguised violence of the southern night.

When Marie Bannerman is later found dead, her murder is first blamed on the Negro maid, then on the Negro who is being hunted in the swamp, and finally on "any darky at all" (*Bits of Paradise* 149). At last, the narrator uncovers proof that Catherine Jones has committed the murder out of jealousy, another instance of human action controlled by ungoverned feeling. The narrator marries and moves to New York, where the periodic crime waves are less terrifying than the violence of the southern small towns. Significantly, in Fitzgerald's description, the southern small town is "unknowable" and "incalculable," "secret" and "opaque." Its nature is as dark as one imagines life in the depths of the sea, and equally disturbing.[5]

Fitzgerald's conception of the South, particularly his characterization of the southern belle, is developed more fully in *The Great Gatsby* than in any of his short stories. Jordan Baker's account of Daisy stresses the typical belle motifs: her social standing, popularity, and flirtatiousness. "The largest of the banners [red, white and blue banners for the Fourth of July] belonged to Daisy Fay's house. She was just eighteen, two years older than me, and by far the most popular of all the young girls in Louisville. She dressed in white, and had a little white roadster, and all day long the telephone rang in her house and excited young officers from Camp Taylor demanded the privilege of monopolizing her that night" (*Bodley Head* 1: 75). As Gatsby reveals to Nick just before he is killed by Wilson, he was attracted to Daisy because she was exciting and mysterious, a sensual and perhaps decadent presence that briefly comes into contact with his life of mundane commercial striving. Strangely voyeuristic, Gatsby is "excited…that many men had already loved Daisy." Nick comments sardonically that "he didn't realize just how extraordinary a 'nice' girl could be" (*Bodley Head* 1: 148–49).

Daisy's role as imagined dream is symbolic of the failure of America itself: the American continent now entirely tamed and transformed into "inessential houses," no longer "commensurate to [the dreamer's] capacity for wonder" (*Bodley Head* 1: 182). The ideal of the Old South that Fitzgerald once associated with the belle has been subsumed by a figure associated with crass opportunism, a figure of the southern belle as representative of the national rapprochement between the commercial North and the New South. Tom, only after the briefest consideration, includes Daisy as a member of his "Nordic" circle, a significant refiguration of the belle as a new ally of the national mission. In Fitzgerald's eyes, of course, it is the final betrayal of the southern dream. What is significant is that now, rather than stressing the opposition of North and South, Fitzgerald has aligned the belle almost completely with the northern mercenary identity.

This linkage of the narcissistic and the mercenary is the key to understanding Fitzgerald's presentation of the belle and his conception of the New South in general. At the heart of the belle character is a self-centeredness that results in a lack of concern for others. It is hardly surprising that her nervousness, a quality associated with the belle's flirtatiousness, should result directly in the death of Mrs. Wilson and indirectly in that of Gatsby. Still, even with his "faint doubt" awakened, Gatsby is held by Daisy's voice, "with its fluctuating, feverish warmth, because it couldn't be over-dreamed—that voice was a deathless song" (*Bodley Head* 1: 97). Clearly, neither Gatsby nor Nick can ever really get beyond the seductive manipulativeness of Daisy's voice, as when she arrives at Gatsby's party with Tom, her voice filled with what the narrator perceives as "tricks." Her voice, so full of warmth and excitement but lacking in any definite meaning, is emblematic of the South's betrayal of its role in the nation's psychic economy, its failure to remain the dream of aristocracy and social grace uncorrected by commerce. The hidden meaning that Gatsby uncovers is crucial: her voice is not only imprudent and reckless, as Nick realizes, but filled with the suggestion of money.

It was the same sense of dangerous unprincipled seductiveness that Fitzgerald came to associate with Zelda, but while Fitzgerald's biographical experience inevitably influenced his southern narratives, his literary and cultural background was a more important influence, so much so that it shaped his attitudes toward the South and, one imagines, his expectations in his marriage to Zelda Sayre. Rather than viewing Fitzgerald's literary production as the reflection of his personal experience, we would do well to read his personal experience as, to a large extent, the product of contemporary attitudes toward the South that he acquired from popular magazines and other media. Fitzgerald's southern fiction adapts many elements of popular stereotypes of the South, and, in doing so, he reworks the conventional motifs for his own purposes, developing a coherent and quite critical conception of the New South. While his southern fiction touches upon certain biographical elements, its main purpose is to develop a critique of the modern South and, more broadly, a critique of the cynical materialism that Fitzgerald perceived in American society generally in the 1920s. At the center of this critique is the figure of the belle, important not so much because of her representation of Zelda Sayre Fitzgerald as for what she reveals about the duplicitous naiveté of America's newly affluent class, whether in the North or in the South. In Fitzgerald's writing, the figure of the belle is employed as a representative of the lost innocence not of a single woman but of an entire civilization.

Notes

1   In particular, the South was idealized for its assumed "strength." As Robert A. Armour points out, in his pioneering films D. W. Griffith had portrayed the way in which "the innate dignity and grace...allowed [southerners] to survive the war and Reconstruction" (20). Later, following the market crash of 1929, the nation sought models of endurance and strong character, and with the familiar motifs of the ruined plantation, of impoverishment and disease, and with the great flood of 1927 in recent memory, the South become the setting for many stories of survival.

The focus on "survival" as a southern trait was widespread. As J. P. Telotte shows, John Ford, best known for his powerful Westerns, directed a series of important southern films, including at least four silent films produced between 1918 and 1925. Telotte believes that, lacking a personal connection with the South, Ford "turned to the prevalent myths and stereotypes of the South," specifically to certain familiar character types (120). In Ford's depiction, southerners are agrarian and individualistic but at the same time "uprooted from the land, almost alienated from the world they continue to inhabit" (121). In this view, southerners are essentially traditionalists struggling to make sense of a world in which their values have been displaced by the effects of the Civil War and Reconstruction. Southern men are noble but "futile" in their resistance to change (121–22). Despite Ford's sympathy for these characters, he depicts them as "outsiders" and "in a vacuum." Anachronistic yet enduring, Ford's southerners are admirable because they represent "the human spirit...which persists in clinging to and fashioning something of worth" (122), even in the face of defeat. Several of Ford's southern films from the mid-1930s featured Will Rogers, an actor who had already come to represent a particular southern type in the minds of the American public: "the image of a wise, down-to-earth type, mindful and respectful of the past, yet aware of and involved in the present" (124). One of the important cultural assumptions implied in this figure is the idea of "personal strength and resourcefulness" as the product of and antidote to the bewildering force of historical change. Set in the 1890s, the films *Judge Priest* and *Steamboat 'Round the Bend* depict the South at a crucial historical juncture: the point at which the devastating effects of the Civil War were still impacting the region but at which one could imagine strong characters such as the Will Rogers persona in a heroic struggle for survival (Telotte 129–30).

2   The impoverished Virginian was a staple of popular fiction. In Jesse Sprague's "An American Banker," a *Post* story of 4 February 1928, an impoverished Virginia aristocrat works his way to the top of the New York banking profession. The impoverished aristocrat also appears in Fitzgerald's "The Popular Girl," a *Post* story (11 and 18 February 1922).

3   Most critics of Fitzgerald's southern stories have focused on the image of the southern belle and on the biographical sources of Fitzgerald's writing, particularly on his troubled relationship with Zelda Sayre Fitzgerald. See, among others, C. Hugh Holman, Scott Donaldson, and John Kuehl. Holman is especially insightful in relating the belle to her role within a traditional social order that would have appealed to "the Northern outsider" (60).

4   One of the associated ideas in Fitzgerald's writing is that of the mysterious "facade" of ruined or decaying plantation homes: the recruits rarely penetrate the facade and enter the southern home. Instead, they are met at the door by black housekeepers and entertained by the belle on the veranda, not in the parlor. There is the assumption of something hidden, a secret corruption, incest, or madness that lies within.

5   Zelda's stories provide a witty and often acerbic but significantly less damning description of small-town existence in the South. "Southern Girl" (*College Humor* October 1929) describes the town of Jeffersonville: "Nothing seems ever to happen in Jeffersonville; the days pass, lazily gossiping in the warm sun. A lynching, an election, a wedding, catastrophes and business booms all take on the same value, rounded, complete, dusted by the lush softness of the air in a climate too hot for any but sporadic effort, too beneficent for any but the most desultory competition" (*Bits of Paradise* 219). In this story, Harriet, the "southern girl," meets Louise when the latter stays at her mother's boarding house. Harriet immediately recognizes that Louise is not a southern girl: her hair is black and "too sleek" and her "dark clothes" are too carefully tailored to be of southern production.

5

James Agee's Radical Honesty

Despite the resurgence of interest in his writing, James Agee will never be considered a major American writer. This was not for lack of talent, and certainly not for lack of ambition. Agee possessed more stylistic and technical ability than Theodore Dreiser, for example, a writer who despite his pedestrian and sometimes boorish qualities (Agee wrote that Dreiser in *An American Tragedy* is "horribly obvious, and has no humor" [qtd. in Bergreen 44]), remains one of the major writers of the modern period. Agee's command of language and intellectual sophistication exceeded those of Dreiser, and his passion for social justice was perhaps equal as well, and yet in comparison with his predecessor, Agee is distinctly a minor figure. What exactly was missing?

We can begin by thinking about the nature of Dreiser's accomplishment, which was, I believe, to have written fiction that is supported by an unshakeable conviction in the moral truth of what it represents. By this, I do not mean simply that his novels proceed from a naturalistic aesthetic in which narrative is tied to the level of everyday experience. More significant is the sense of purposefulness underlying Dreiser's fiction: from beginning to end, his absorbing tales of greed, ambition, and self-delusion are held together by a coherent vision of what is and is not permissible within the uncharted moral universe that his characters traverse. Even as Sister Carrie and Jennie Gerhardt lose their bearings, the author and reader work to restore order to a social world whose ethics is ambiguous and conflicted. The fate of Carrie or Jennie, or, for that matter, of Clyde Griffiths, concerns the reader because of the possibility of their tragic moral failure—a failure that can only be conceived in light of the assumed existence of an objective shared standard of moral success. Dreiser's protagonists lose sight of, betray, but never actually disavow the inherited code of values that they have brought with them to the modern urban wasteland. Their tragic fall from grace always seems an inevitability resulting from the equivocal moral choices of actors who are oblivious to the consequences of their actions. Because of its "accidental" and progressive nature, Dreiser's evil appears as something that might befall any of his readers, a fact that makes his stories all the more evocative. Still, the process by which Dreiser's protagonists have failed is clearly understood by the author and the reader.

In contrast, there is not a single character in Agee's canon that we care about so deeply. Agee's souls are truly equivocal, lost but not actually tragic, and none of them could be us, for they reside outside the common realm of moral experience of most readers. Reading Agee's tales of childhood loss is like reading what happens to Medea's forgotten children. Rufus Follet is a strange and atypical character, not a representative one, and unlike Sister Carrie, who rouses the reader's concern and interest even as she disappoints one's expectations, Rufus evokes little empathy. A tragedy is set in motion with the "inevitable" automobile accident—inevitable given the unique series of causes that are carefully spelled out including the father's probable drunken condition—and the tragedy is compounded by the cruel remoteness of response of Rufus' mother and her relations and by the inability of anyone, even the sympathetic Aunt Hannah, to proffer real assistance. The result is the seemingly irreversible damage, already evident at the age of six, to a child's soul. It is a quirky tragedy of fate and of human estrangement—the "one in a million" chance of the cotter pin and the bloodless injury and the cruel lack of sympathy in the Follet household—but, unless we share these very unusual circumstances, it is nothing to us.

A Death in the Family is an autobiographical novel focused on a troubled and already defeated childhood persona of Agee. As a result, the novel is static and constricted, for the true center of interest in the work is the evolution of a fearful, self-absorbed personality. It is just the sort of fictional persona that Jacques Maritain warned of in *The Responsibility of the Artist*: the romantic artist figure whose creation replaces a balanced vision of ordinary human experience with the narcissistic focus on the artist himself. The author of such autobiographical fiction "unloads himself" in his work, "pours his own complexes and poisons into it" (54), and in so doing he sacrifices the values of art to his own egotism or need for therapy. As Maritain shows, this romantic artist persona evolved into a more complex but hardly less destructive figuration during the Modernist period as the romantic hero was transformed into a priestly figure who, largely as a result of his more acute conscience, found himself alienated even further from the crass materialism of bourgeois society. For such a figure, society's indifference and ingratitude seemed to engender his increasing alienation from it and to justify his attitude of cynicism and supercilious contempt. A similar development from idealistic rebel to embittered cynic is all too apparent in Agee's case. As

Laurence Bergreen stresses, Agee felt that by definition the artist must confront society and suffer at its hands, "sacrific[ing] whatever was dearest to him" (372).

Agee adopted and carried to an extreme the modernist ethos that Maritain had warned of, the idea that the artist was the godlike creator of the future consciousness of the race, yet such an aesthetic had become antiquated by the time Agee happened upon it. During the 1940s, the prime of his creative life, Agee had little to say to a world that was enduring the greatest ordeal in human history, and Agee's relative silence concerning World War II and the Holocaust was one symptom of just how out of joint his aesthetic was. In contrast with emerging postwar writers including Saul Bellow and Flannery O' Connor, Agee came to seem even more irrelevant because he turned away from the major crises of his times—not just the historical devastation but the spiritual failure that underlay it. This very irrelevance compounds the irony of the critical reception of his posthumous novel, *A Death in the Family*, focused as it was on the book's seeming nostalgia and domesticity, qualities that might seem attractive in the aftermath of a global conflict. Agee set his major works in the early decades of the twentieth century not for nostalgic reasons but as a way of favoring a conception of reality that was essentially personal and aesthetic over the political and historical. In fact, he made no imaginative response to what had taken place since the beginning of World War II, and his response to the Great Depression was also highly idiosyncratic.

Even in *Famous Men*, Agee can be seen fleeing from historical experience into a cocoon that involves his imagined reunion with a southern family long lost to him. George and Annie Mae Gudger become surrogate parents, while the context of the tenant subject matter, rather than immersing Agee in the Depression-era crisis of agrarian poverty, removes him from the actual conflicts of his day. This is not only because by the time he finished work on the book—conceived in 1936 but not published until 1941—public interest in the topic of sharecropping had all but vanished in anticipation of America's entry into the war; it was also because Agee never perceived the lives of the tenant families to be "in crisis." Agee focused on the classic "beauty" of the tenant way of life rather than on its impoverishment. Because of the extreme "simplicity" of their lives, he viewed them as fortunate exceptions to the poisonous materialism of American bourgeois society. The liberal script of social uplift generally followed by the sharecropper narratives of the 1930s conflicted with Agee's more essential script, one in which the tenant families were not victims but in a sense privileged by virtue of their exclusion from middle-class society. The radical simplicity of the croppers' lives is immediately made known in the prelude to the book, "On the Porch: 1," in which Agee makes it clear that the three families are living, to a large extent, outside the influence of human society, yet, in just such a life, at the mercy of all manner of natural and economic forces but beyond the assistance of society, Agee finds a model for the self-abandonment and forlorn release of the self that he aspires to achieve in his own life. In Agee's view, the desolate lives of the tenants are not candidates for public assistance but are envied models of deprivation and simplicity.

While Agee seeks to join the tenants in their impoverishment, at the same time he seeks a kind of riches that are beyond their reach. In fact, the true scale of his ambition is immense, as is apparent from the section "A Country Letter" in which Agee speaks of sitting in the cabin at night by the light of a kerosene lamp. If one remains still enough, he says, he can tell "anything within realm of God, whatsoever it may be" (*Famous Men* 49). What Agee suggests is a creation that is as original in its own way as that of any of the "artists" that he names as "greater men" than himself, a list that includes Blake, Joyce, Kafka, Beethoven, and Christ himself. Agee's goal is to express ineffable truths about all of humanity that have never been expressed before, as when he considers the frailty and remoteness of the sharecropper settlement, tiny beneath the wide night sky. The focus on three tenant families, apparently the most humble of subjects, is deceptive, since Agee intends to make these families icons not so much of the condition of human beings generally as of the highest ambition of the human race—that is, the relinquishment of physical existence altogether.

To advance an ideological subversion of convention, it is crucial that Agee's sharecroppers not be presented as *ordinary* human beings: they are "holy," they are saints, George is Christ, and Annie Mae the Madonna. Conceived in these terms from the beginning, the Gudgers can be viewed as paragons of virtue, but what of the majority of human beings who are not saintly by virtue of their victimization? In Agee's scheme, the vast majority of human beings—those ordinary middle-class citizens from Agee's own background—come across as desperate cases of hypocrisy and irremediable corruption. In this maneuver, Agee was employing a familiar device of radical rhetoric, a form of bifurcation in which one's own familiar culture is judged wanting by contrast with the mythical virtues of a remote culture about which the veracity of one's report must be accepted on faith. His intention is to hold up to the middle class the fact that sharecroppers can be more "honest" and more spiritual than itself. It is as if Agee wished to condemn the human race by reporting the existence of a more virtuous and long-suffering race of beings on some distant planet. Conveniently, it would be impossible for critics to check the veracity of his report and thus difficult to challenge his argument.

Agee's sense of himself and of his relation to the great spiritual leaders of mankind is also suggested by his overblown notion of the holiness of the three tenant families that he encounters in Alabama. As Alan Spiegel rightly points out, the farmers with whom Agee closely identifies are themselves envisaged, not as representative men and women but as "avatars and legatees of famous men" (142). By any conventional standard, and certainly by the standard of the townspeople with whom Agee and Walker Evans speak, the three families on whom they decide to focus their efforts are not avatars of famous men but rather are among the least respectable in the community. They are regarded by their fellow citizens as lazy, shiftless, and immoral, and yet Agee depicts them as holy vessels, not merely equal to the townspeople but far superior to them in spiritual terms.

Agee's ambition in *Famous Men* is not primarily a quest for identity, the central motive that many readers have perceived in the book, but rather, as in almost everything he wrote, the subversion of the bourgeois culture against which he had set himself early in life. In the service of this task, Agee strains to infuse his narration of an often coarse subject matter with the splendor of biblical image and language. Even as he documents many of these instances, from Agee's use of the Forty-third Psalm to convey his feelings toward the holiness of the Gudger house to his depiction of George Gudger as a Christ-figure in overalls and of Annie Mae Gudger as a hard-bitten Madonna, James Lowe fails to note the disparity between this employment of Christian references and what Lowe himself characterizes as "a conflict between belief and disbelief in God" (114). Even Agee's conception of crucifixion, a trope that he employs frequently in the book, is one that undermines rather than supports Christian belief. As Agee says, Christ's own three hours on the cross were "too trivial an emblem" of the sufferings of ordinary human beings (*Famous Men* 92). It is the living who experience the real crucifixion, not the mythological figure of Christ.

Implicit in Agee's conception of aesthetics is the sense that the artist, rejected by the smug morality of the middle class—as he believes himself to be—no longer performs a public role; he is now at the mercy of society, with which he plays the part required of him, whether this be the innocuous entertainer or the fashionable theorist. In Agee's case, the point is that he performed this social role more willingly than he ever imagined, ultimately becoming a cult figure after his death but accomplishing little by his writing. Rebellion and self-punishment matched the social expectations of what the young, post-romantic soul should resemble, but they failed to claim a public role for the artist, something that Faulkner or Naipaul may be said to have done. What Agee's rebellion confirmed was precisely what society wished to see in its artists: an entertaining spectacle of little consequence in terms of challenging the actual dominance of society itself.

In *The Human Condition*, Hannah Arendt discusses the effects of the subsuming of the private and public spheres of life into the "social," a hybrid mode of experience that dominates modern existence. With the loss of both the private and the public realms as distinct domains, modern man lives within a homogeneous, all-encompassing social realm in which private experience is no longer private but controlled by a pervasive consciousness of social norms and behavioral expectations, and in which public life is no longer the arena of political activity but of a single-minded politics controlled by public opinion and propagandistic rhetoric. "Seen from this viewpoint," Arendt writes, "the modern discovery of intimacy seems a flight from the whole outer world into the inner subjectivity of the individual, which formerly had been sheltered and protected by the private realm" (211). Certainly, the confessional quality of Agee's writing—the intimate scenes of family life in *A Death in the Family*, the embarrassing admissions of physical attraction to Emma Woods in *Let Us Now Praise Famous Men*, the revelations of failure and transgression throughout his correspondence with Father Flye—reveal an author drawn to self-revelation, an autobiographical method of "total commitment to his own experience" that Alfred T. Barson assumes to be a normative quality of all art (78). While the hazards of this method are not recognized by Barson and were certainly never totally apparent to Agee, the fact is that an unwavering focus on the self and on the revelation of intimacy has significant ethical implications.

If one part of Agee's work points us toward a struggle against the injustices of the world—the issues of social equality and suffering that dominate *Let Us Now Praise Famous Men* and much of his journalistic writing—another and larger part of his writing displays a narcissistic focus. Preoccupation with personal freedom and individual rights leads Agee away from a consideration of the general conditions of human life that in the classical and Christian traditions comprise the basis of an ethical consensus. Aristotle began the *Ethics* by questioning the nature of human happiness, thus setting in motion a philosophical inquiry concerning the "good" for human beings that occupied the Western ethical tradition from the Greeks through the Victorians, but that has been increasingly lost sight of in modern consciousness. Charles Dickens, whose work may be taken as a proxy of the Victorian morality that Agee was rebelling against, retained at least some sense of the reality of private and public worlds that Arendt has articulated. The conclusion of *Little Dorrit*, certainly among the most didactic of Dickens' novels, offers an explicit declaration of what the Victorians might regard as the "good" in life: as they leave the church where they have been married, Amy and Arthur Clennam go "down into a modest life of usefulness and happiness" (895), a life filled with a mother's care for children, tenderness for Amy's misguided brother, and, of course, on Arthur's part, enterprise in his business partnership of Doyce and Clennam. "Inseparable" and "blessed" with one another's love, Arthur and Amy, with their abiding sense of duty, enter into a world of chaos, selfishness, and vanity, but by their effort and faith they intend to redeem this fallen world, at least to the extent to which they are able.

Nothing like this exists in Agee's writing. As James Lowe correctly notes of *Famous Men*, Agee's narrative involves a "consistent emphasis on asymmetry—disparateness as a basis for unity that cuts across aesthetic, religious, and economic boundaries" (118). The conclusion of *A Death in the Family*, following immediately upon the funeral of Rufus' father, is shadowed by uncertainty and fear rather than by the sort of comfort and solidarity that one might wish for him. Walking with Uncle Andrew, Rufus has entered a harsh and uncertain world, but he possesses no cultural resources for improving this world. In place of Dickens' blessed home, filled with love and devotion to duty, Agee inserts a domestic space blasted by anger and suspicion. In place of purposeful labor, there is only the prospect of bohemian rebellion along the lines suggested by Uncle Andrew; in place of a humble and responsible relation to others, there is already in Rufus a tendency toward withdrawal and self-absorption.

One should realize that Agee's conception of the family is related in a crucial sense to his social ethics; indeed, one necessitates the other. Arendt points to "the striking coincidence of the rise of society with the decline of the family," that is, "the absorption of the family unit into corresponding social groups" (192). As Arendt suggests, within this distinctly modern development, the figure of the *pater familias* that once governed the private realm is supplanted by social opinion and increasingly by behavioral norms and conformity. The "death" in the family—not the loss of a particular father but the loss of the traditional governance of the family by the *pater familias*—is, after all, Agee's primary concern, although one can hardly imagine Jay Follet's ever having served as a *pater familias*. What haunts Agee is not the personal loss but the much larger question of what takes the place of the paternal role within modern society: the rule of society through the mechanism of mass media, social functions and expectations, and bureaucracy. Far from securing a new degree of freedom, this enlargement of society imposes a far-reaching control over human personality, subsuming as it does the private and the public spheres within what Arendt terms the new "hybrid" sphere of the "social." Symbolically represented in the particular events of the novel is the displacement of an order of private and public life by the social: the supplanting of a mode of existence that is still relatively free by a new order of equality that imposes severe restrictions on human action. Within this new order, as Arendt argues, it is assumed that human beings "unanimously followed certain patterns of behavior, so that those who did not keep the rules could be considered to be asocial or abnormal." The result is that "everything that is not everyday behavior or automatic trends has been ruled out as immaterial" (194).

The sense of unreality that exists in the Follet household following the father's death evidences the dominance of the social order. Events are suddenly swept up by an automatic ritual of expected behavior; freedom of expression is curtailed; human beings become deadly automatons voicing scripts composed of clichés. Understandably, only phenomena from outside both the private and the public realm—the appearance of Jay's ghost or the butterfly's emergence from Jay's grave—possess the authority to interrupt this sinister decline, but, significantly, from the perspective of the adult consensus, these phenomena are illusory or highly doubtful, and they possess no lasting power to challenge the new order that has descended over the family, or for that matter over the world at large as Rufus experiences it. Perhaps the greatest irony of the situation is that the relinquishment of human freedom is made possible by the influence of a form of social control that operates in the guise of religious practice and is, therefore, all the more difficult to refute. With the social conformity that reigns in the Follet household, freedom of expression—such as Rufus' choice of a sporty, loud cap over a more conventional model—is under attack. More importantly, morally courageous action, such as Rufus' instinctual defense of his father's reputation against the accusations of the older boys, is deemed improper and is quickly curtailed as Rufus is ordered to remain inside, but what this "remaining inside" entails is not the protection that was once assumed to exist within the "private" sphere but the restraint of human freedom consistent with the extension of the social order.

The dominance of the social order helps to explain the central, reflexive motive of Agee's career: his attack on middle-class values. This controlling obsession implied an ironic and subversive mode for his writing, one that has led critics, rightly enough, to associate Agee's work with surrealism, anarchism, and the literature of alienation. In the wake of postmodernism and deconstruction, we can perceive Agee's significance as a precursor of an art of absence in which satire, self-doubt, travesty, and vulnerability are central features, and we can understand how Agee recognized the importance of Kafka as perhaps his own most important predecessor with his insistence on the ineffable nature of art. Intuitively, and well ahead of his time, Agee understood the point of Barthes' critique of authorship and of Foucault's analysis of power, which is why Agee published his writing with the greatest reluctance, insisting at one point that his masterpiece, *Let Us Now Praise Famous Men*, be published on newsprint so that it would vanish in fifty years. From his posture of self-censorship and self-doubt, Agee turned a critical eye on all assertions of value. Only self-contempt can hint at the degree of abnegation that Agee equates with the honest truth. Thus, the positive value of all conventional forms of affiliation is questioned in Agee's thinking, whether this be the affiliation of family, work, patriotism, identification with one's group, pride in one's local community, love of nature, or the valuing of one's religion. Romantic love is also scorned, and there is not a single unqualified depiction of it in Agee's fiction. Because all of these forms of affiliation reflect a pleasure in life that cannot be permitted in the face of the world's suffering, Agee feels compelled to submit them to satire, travesty, and belittlement.

The essential problem with such an idealistic attitude is simply that it does not fit the human condition as it is. It cannot participate in the social and political life because it does not understand what is valued by ordinary people and it does not comprehend the ethical problems of everyday life. The destructive side of Agee's idealism comes across in a number of passages, as in the account of his flirtatious relationship with Emma Woods, Annie Mae's younger sister. Spiegel views Agee's lust as only a stage in his moral development, "the camouflage for a deeper, more generalized, less focused, but, in Agee's case, more telling erotic longing and melancholia" (103), but, in so doing, he deflects judgment from the harmful behavior in which Agee is actually engaged. In fact, Spiegel appears to view this unrestrained appetitiveness in the same manner that Agee himself did—as somehow necessary to his art. In *Famous Men*, Emma is married to an older man who has taken up residence on a remote farm in Mississippi and who has sent for his wife to join him, much against her wishes. In place of the dignified concern that one might expect toward an unhappy woman in her condition, Agee interjects a sexual fantasy. As he says, "there is tenderness and sweetness and mutual pleasure in such a 'flirtation' which one would not for the world restrain or cancel" (*Famous Men* 58). Although nothing comes of his relationship to Emma, what *might* come of it is made clear. Agee's "flirtation," in fact, is not all tenderness and sweetness, since it involves his rejection of a greater good, the potential for a moment of profound empathy devoted to the shared recognition of the sacrifice that all life embodies, rather than to a fruitless physical attraction, something akin to Faust's seduction of Margaret. (Indeed, is not the fantasized seduction of Emma at the most vulnerable point in her life a Faustian act? Is not *Faust* an important intertextual key to *Famous Men* and to much of Agee's artistic career?) In place of noble concern for another human being in tragic straits, Agee pursues a sexual fantasy that he mistakenly believes allows Emma and himself a kind of "mutual pleasure." In the car, as Agee drives Emma and her family members to Cookstown, Agee's flesh is pressed against Emma's. At this moment, Agee is driving Emma to what may be her doom, as she is about to depart for a "hopeless" future with her mean-spirited and jealous husband, and yet what is passing through Agee's mind during the fifteen-minute drive is the physical attraction between their sweating bodies. Evil, as Thomistic theology has it, is the absence of good: in his relationship to Emma Woods, Agee engages in evil not because he entertains a cheap fantasy of seduction but because he willfully avoids the good that he might perform.

But why does he avoid the good that he might otherwise perform? The answer, I believe, lies in Agee's rejection of convention and his hostility toward inherited traditions of belief. As Spiegel points out, Agee's "fully articulated social and artistic position" was stated in his response to a *Partisan Review* questionnaire that he included as the "Intermission" section in *Famous Men*. In his reply, Agee "segregates himself from all institutions, groups, movements, legislation, ideologies, parties, and programs...indeed, from the very idea of society itself" (Spiegel 136). This program of repudiation leaves Agee stranded in an ethical desert with no access to the redeeming influence of major belief systems, in place of which Agee's writing relies to a great degree on what Hannah Arendt terms the "rhetoric of compassion," the cynical deployment of human necessity as a prop in one's argumentation. Agee's writing makes frequent use of tropes of special pleading, and the central figures in his writing—the poor, the children, and the minorities—play an important rhetorical role by virtue of their irrefutable embodiment of suffering. The implication of this rhetoric is that its arguments, because of the supreme reality of its human subject, are beyond appeal and even beyond discussion. Agee's use of the rhetoric of compassion, of course, resembles that which appeared in a wide range of progressive literature from the 1930s and which continued to be deployed with ever-increasing frequency in subsequent decades, but while Agee employed a similar rhetoric for his own purposes, he did not align himself with Marxist politics. From the point of view of most progressives, Agee was simply a nonconformist fellow traveler, one who either lacked the courage of his convictions or whose convictions were muddled by his quaint concern for the welfare of individual human beings. In fact, class warfare, which implies faith in an ultimate "victory" of revolutionary change, was not at all what Agee has in mind: rather it was an elegiac attitude toward life that implied not progress but social dissolution and chaos.

As Richard Porton has written of Agee's politics, "he was far from an orthodox Popular Frontist and, conversely, his 'radical humanism' always appears to be the product of an extended dialog with the reigning political tendencies of the Forties left—liberalism, Stalinism, and Trotskyism" (4). Porton's phrase, "extended dialog," suggests Agee's wariness of political ideologies, and, in fact, he was never a full-fledged convert to any political philosophy. From his student days, Agee lacked interest entirely in practical politics, preferring to think in terms of idealistic conceptions of communal self-government or libertarian individualism. At the height of Marxism's popularity in the mid-1930s, Agee wrote in "Art for What's Sake?" (which appeared in the December 1936 issue of the left-wing *New Masses*) that social revolution in and of itself was not a sufficient basis for the creation of art: art must combine personal, unconscious, and surrealistic qualities with social purposes.

Throughout his lifetime, Agee found communism attractive in many respects, but "belatedly" he rejected it as "only another church, with its own forms of sin and penance" (Bergreen 243). However misguided, Marxism promised not only a more just economic system but also a form of spiritual emancipation through the identification of the individual with the group. Although Agee was uneasy with collectivist thinking of any kind, he was responding to and reacting against many of the same philosophical influences as the Marxism of the 1930s, and he was seeking a similarly utopian redemption. Nonetheless, Agee's view of communism was more ambivalent than that of many of his contemporaries. Even a political system that promised utopian equality was too regimented for Agee. His independence from ideology, his avoidance of political labels, and his championship of personal freedom made him a precursor of libertarianism, a political position that would gain increasing support in the decades after his death but that, like much in Agee's political philosophy, dated back to the period of the French Revolution.

Though Agee has been characterized in many different ways, from a social revolutionary to an essentially religious writer, it was probably closer to the truth, as he wrote Father Flye on 28 June 1938, that he was "essentially an anarchist" (*Letters* 100). In this long letter from Frenchtown, New Jersey, Agee explains that any attempt to "work within" what he views as the corrupt institutions of "the human situation at the worst that it is" is a form of "compromise" (101). Agee trusts only the "Absolutist" who seeks the absolute with "complete disregard for the structures of the world or of living as it [is]" (101). Depicting himself as a heroic figure who cannot know "the difference between right and wrong" and who ventures "beyond the safety of rules" (103), Agee declares that he distrusts not merely politics but all human institutions, and, in particular, Agee singles out the "social" and "religious structures and conceptions" governing marriage and sexuality, which are "evil beyond imagination" (104). "I know that I believe above all," Agee writes, "in joy and in purity and fearlessness of soul" (104). He is one who strives for "goodness" and "true thinking" (104).

To understand this sensibility, we must locate it within an anarchist tradition that can be traced back through Proudhon and Godwin to its intellectual origins in the philosophy of Jean-Jacques Rousseau. In Agee's case, anarchism involved a rejection of all forms of institutionalized religion, all political systems and social ideologies, and all inherited traditions, except, of course, the anarchist tradition itself. These forms of negation were accompanied by belief in the original goodness of human nature before its corruption by society (based on the existence of certain moral instincts: essential values of honesty, fairness, and equality), and a demand for complete personal freedom. Agee's anarchism, however, should be distinguished from that of his predecessors in that it lacked the programmatic aspects of Bakunin's activism or of Proudhon's collectivist theories. Agee's thinking tended toward a radical individualism under which, as he wrote in connection with the bombing of Hiroshima, "each man is eternally and above all else responsible for his own soul" (qtd. in Bergreen 295). Following the utopian philosophy of Saint-Simon and Auguste Comte, Agee argued that social rules and traditions of belief were based, at best, on arbitrary criteria, and, as a consequence, he promoted society's total reorganization based on a radical destruction of social forms and a return to individual conscience. Lacking the conviction of earlier anarchists, however, Agee had little confidence that social change could actually be brought about, and, perhaps as a result of his lack of conviction, his ideas—they can hardly be called a "program" for change—consisted of a series of impassioned pleas for greater honesty or conscience or martyrdom.

It is extraordinary to read Agee's anarchist declaration to Father Flye if we consider that it was written in the summer of 1938. By this time, Hitler had risen to power; the persecution of Jews and others had begun in earnest; Mussolini had invaded Ethiopia; the second Sino-Japanese War had begun with the invasion of Manchuria; and within months much of Czechoslovakia would be ceded to Hitler in the Munich Pact. In other words, the world was already launched on its way toward the horrific destruction that would claim at least fifty million lives by the end of World War II, and, yet, Agee is speaking of an ethical capitulation and an escape into a dreamland of personal freedom and sexual gratification. One might claim that like a majority of Americans, Agee simply did not perceive the gravity of events, but the fact is that even by the end of the war, Agee had not changed his position. He viewed the entry of the United States into World War II as immoral, and on 30 October 1943 he wrote Father Flye that the postwar era that he envisioned following an allied victory would be "little better in most respects (if we get our way) than Hitler would bring" (*Letters* 138). As Bergreen put it, "the conflict failed to inspire a deep personal response in Agee. Often he wished it would simply blow away" (265), but in the wartime context, Agee's remarks seem not only foolish but cynical and immoral as well. At a moment when millions of civilians were suffering the persecutions of fascism and millions of combatants were risking their lives to liberate them, Agee was astoundingly shallow and self-centered. His failure ever to respond to the war or to the Holocaust with anything like an appropriate gravity unmasks a decisive moral failing grounded in qualities of megalomania and narcissism. So great was Agee's absorption with the personal drama of "Agee" that he was unable to comprehend the significance of reality outside himself.

Nonetheless, there was one issue that did engage Agee's imagination and that led him toward commitment of a sort. The inability of so-called rational men to control the technology that their own reason had created was a problem that troubled Agee deeply, especially during the 1940s, yet even his concern over the harmful effects of technology did not lead him to consider the necessity of participation in practical politics. Agee's essay entitled "Victory, the Peace: The Bomb," published in *Time* on 20 August 1945, just two weeks after the bombing of Hiroshima, is his most impassioned statement of the problem, yet this essay points once again to a radical dismissal of human institutions. At the heart of Agee's skepticism lies one of the fundamental motives of his life: a rebellion against the religious framework of beliefs of his mother and against the middle-class culture of her family. It was a rejection of conventional life that bordered on paranoia, for Agee was not able to accept the fact that ordinary human beings can simply be good. Agee's contempt for his own class, it turns out, was the central motive in his life. It influenced his behavior in many respects, from his lack of confidence in his own writing, his indecisiveness, his failed marriages, to his relation to employers and teachers. This self-hatred was the working out of Agee's feelings of guilt for the death of his father, the sense that he had failed or betrayed his father but also the sense that he was unloved by his mother, and yet Agee was not the first young man ever to lose his father or to sense that he was not adequately loved. What is unusual in his case is the extent to which these feelings dominated his life and the way in which they so neatly fit into the entire worldview that Agee constructed. One could say that Agee's sense of personal rejection and lack of family love was turned outward to contain the entire world. If there were no worthwhile acceptance in the family, there could be no acceptance within any other human group or institution. If Agee must be doomed by virtue of his lack of acceptance within the family, the world might as well be doomed, also. In Agee's mind, modern civilization as a whole resembled a family that had lost its bearings and in its disintegration was sacrificing its children on the altar of capitalism and institutionalized religion. Clearly, for Agee there was no solution to this societal doom. Western civilization as a whole could not be healed. There were only instants of reprieve, moments of escape such as the weeks he spent with the Alabama tenants.

Such moments of reprieve were rare, and to a great extent Agee lived in despair of ever discovering the quality of freedom that he dreamed of. Not only did he dream of freedom, of course, he seemed to require it, even as it brought him ever closer to the edge of destruction. In "What Is Freedom?" Hannah Arendt points to the familiar misconception that freedom and free will are identical concepts, when, in fact, they are quite opposed. Freedom, which Arendt defines as the capacity for action within the public sphere, has far less to do with the exercise of free will, which is essentially an exercise of personal power rather than a productive engagement with others. Agee's exaggerated willfulness, I believe, helps to explain the fact that, as Agee himself admitted on several occasions, he was more certain of what he opposed than of what he advocated. Agee was especially prone to what Elias Canetti termed "the pleasure of pronouncing an unfavourable verdict" (*Crowds* 296), a quality that is particularly noticeable in his brief reviews. In the case of Agee, this "disease" of rendering negative judgments was accompanied by an habitual impulse to "unmask" those positions of moral authority that rivaled his own, an impulse that Canetti connects with the grandiose fantasy world of the paranoiac, a fantasy accompanied by the shrinking of the experiential world in which "the wealth of appearances comes to mean nothing" (*Crowds* 378).

It has not been adequately noted, I believe, to what extent Agee was essentially a critic rather than a creative artist per se. The bulk of Agee's writing consists of journalistic prose and reviews, but even his fiction and poems are essentially works of social satire. As Agee himself realized at one point, perhaps his most natural mode of expression was the short review, particularly the film review (Bergreen 269). In the role of the mere reviewer of a popular form of art, he could preach against the failings of the American middle-class culture, a culture closely identified with the Hollywood film, without exposing himself as the heavy-handed moralist that he was. In his review of the film *Mildred Pierce*, for example, "one of the few anywhere near honest ones," Agee praises the "nasty, gratifying version of the James Cain novel" with its "constant, virulent, lambent attention to money and its effects, and more authentic suggestions of sex than one hopes to see in American films" (*Agee on Film* 165). In their own way, all of Agee's reviews implied a similar critique of the ugly "conspiracy" of the middle class to live in comfort and abundance while within the same world others lived in poverty and affliction.

Ultimately, Agee's rebellion led him toward ever-increasing forms of negation—not merely film reviews that lacerated the apathy of the American people or journalistic attacks like *Famous Men* that insisted on the ever-present guilt of everyone alive for the suffering of any. Finally, Agee was led to the paradoxical position that, given the moral responsibility of humanity for all that exists and the impossibility of ever meeting the standards of responsibility that he asserted, no human action could actually be said to be moral. Given this "collapse" of ethics, no human being could be held to account since all conceivable standards of conduct were unworkable anyway. As Agee admitted in "Dream Sequence," the result of his disillusionment was a "convenient lack of convictions" (263) that freed him and everyone else from restrictions of any sort.

In contrast to the great majority of human beings, who find that a lack of convictions is repugnant, Agee wore his moral indecisiveness like a badge of honor. Throughout his career, Agee weighed the possible meanings of faithlessness, pondering the word's relationship to his failed or flawed human relationships and to his art, but he never seems to have understood its commonsense meaning: a lack of belief in overriding principles. From a very early point in his life, Agee's principles were already compromised, so much so that the fundamental virtues of constancy and decency were simply beyond him. Agee's dedication to the truth, his radical honesty, was something that he was willing to die for and that carried him beyond art and life, but the honesty that he practiced was lethal in the demands it made of him. His radical dedication to what he terms "purity" carried Agee and his readers beyond humanity and toward a courtship of death. In Agee's view, since values and institutions were always "tainted" by the compromises that molded them in the first place, honesty required the destruction of everything. Finally, Agee had in mind not merely the destruction of the middle class but of all human institutions, values, and affiliations. Nothing in this world can be holy except for the most demeaned and squalid, those things that in a sense do not exist at all; everything else must be sacrificed to Agee's radical honesty.

6

Wise Blood: O'Connor's Vision of a Broken World

Flannery O'Connor regarded non-believers, especially those pseudo-intellectuals who proclaimed their atheism with assurance, as intellectually narrow and biased. Clearly, the claims of atheism cannot be empirically proved, no more so than the claims of believers. At the very least, as O'Connor wrote Louise Abbot, "If you feel you can't believe, you must at least do this: keep an open mind" (*Habit* 192). Applying this standard, she would have regarded James Agee as among the more closed-minded of her contemporaries. O'Connor was certainly no fan of Agee. Her aversion to his writing was so pronounced, in fact, that she once wrote in an unpublished letter that "after she had read an excerpt from *A Death in the Family*, she knew that she didn't want to read the rest of it" (Cash 241). Certain interesting similarities, however, do exist between the two writers: both were products of deeply religious backgrounds, and both wrote fiction that drew on their religious training in terms of theme, content, and style; both lost their fathers at a young age, and this loss deeply affected their lives and work; both display an extreme sense of the importance of spiritual existence, and, in their pursuit of some ultimate source of belief, both write about martyrdom, but with very different results; finally, to the extent that they suggest a source of amelioration to the damaged lives that they depict, both find it in the transformation of individual human beings rather than in state or collective actions.

At this point, however, the similarities between O'Connor and Agee end. In contrast with the pointless rebellion of Agee's self-destructive protagonists, O'Connor's fiction points toward a relinquishment of secular materialism and a recognition of mystery. In contrast with the hopelessness of Agee's world, in which neither collectivist nor individualistic approaches afford meaningful solutions to the great damage that exists, O'Connor envisages a transformation of individuals that is the product of an acceptance of divine grace. Agee's repeated persona, an autobiographical figure whom he traces through both his fictional and nonfictional works, betrays an awareness of his own spiritual destructiveness but finds himself incapable of seeking a remedy in any form of redemptive belief system. By contrast, O'Connor's persona in *Wise Blood*, Hazel Motes, discovers a source of meaning and wholeness in his devotion to the spiritual life. By immersing himself in tradition, even to the point of martyrdom at the hands of a modernity in which tradition is despised more than anything, Haze achieves realization of the purpose toward which his life has been tending, even for generations before his birth. Agee, on the other hand, essentially seeks forgiveness for the "crime" of continuing to live in a world in which his father no longer exists and in which other human beings lack the privileges that he enjoys as a middle-class American. Since, in fact, Agee can never rid himself of this inheritance, even in his rebellion against it, he can only find perfect atonement in the extinguishing of consciousness. Even though there are intriguing biographical and cultural similarities between James Agee and Flannery O'Connor, Agee's survivor guilt reflects a perspective utterly opposed to that of O'Connor.

Not all critics, of course, have interpreted O'Connor's work as entirely removed from the secular values that Agee appears to have embraced. In a thought-provoking article that focuses on the eschatological vision in *Wise Blood*, Susan Edmunds points to what she refers to as the "anagogical" relationship between sociohistorical and eschatological levels of narrative. In particular, Edmunds is interested in the racial and gendered elements in the novel that, she believes, are informed by the analogy with the Pauline vision of Christ's redemptive Second Coming. This reading is tied together by the many mirror and glass images in the narrative, which Edmunds takes to refer to the verses from *I Cor.* 13: 9–10: "For now we see through a glass darkly; but then face to face...." In this reading, the point of O'Connor's presumed analogy is to suggest, in particular, her championing of racial and gender equality: that is, a focus on the transformation of the sociohistorical level of reality by taking into account the parallel conception of the Second Coming. This was, in fact, a course of action prescribed by Jacques Maritain, a Catholic theologian whom O'Connor read with interest and approval, who wrote that "[t]he temporal task of the Christian world is to work on earth for a socio-temporal realization of the Gospel truths" ("Roots" 256). These truths could be understood as "a very precise ethical code" (256) that was clearly enunciated in the New Testament and has been the shared code of all Christian societies.

Certainly, O'Connor supported tolerance and justice toward all human beings, but the project of social reform is totally absent from her fiction. For O'Connor, the only permanent way to improve human relationships in this world is through the acceptance of the redemptive power of grace. The argument for sociohistorical justice that Edmunds purports to find in *Wise Blood* leads only to frustration and futility and finally to evil. As John Desmond points out, the character of the Misfit in "A Good Man Is Hard to Find" is precisely the type of rationalist, thoroughly grounded in the present, who seeks a perfect accounting for justice in the here and now. The Misfit is one who "cannot admit the need of a power beyond logic and human justice that is, one can believe, more than commensurate to the mystery and power of evil" (130). Essentially, his problem is that of the modern secularist who wishes to find a "solution" to the problem of evil, but since evil is ineradicable—human nature will never be perfected; natural disasters will never be eliminated; disease and death are a permanent part of existence—the secularist can never arrive at a satisfactory "explanation" for the fundamental inequity of the human condition. This inequity, a condition in which the seeming injustice in which we are born can never be explained in rational terms, is an abiding aspect of the human condition that can only be understood as part of a larger order of mystery.

The problem with Edmunds' historicizing is not so much that it misinterprets Pauline scripture altogether as that, in its totalizing application of one emphasis of the scripture, it leads to a distortion of the traditional conception of Catholic existence that O'Connor would have embraced. One aspect of this conception lacking in Edmunds' reading is the crucial knowledge that all human existence in this world is permanently circumscribed by suffering and "clouded" by the mistaken vision of human beings. Only with the coming of Christ at the end of time is the sinful and needful condition in which humans exist fundamentally changed. O'Connor's understanding is somewhat akin to what Robert Frost wrote in the poem, "Provide, Provide." The theme of this poem is the element of necessity that pervades all human existence in terms of both the natural and social evils that humans encounter, accompanied by a deep awareness of the harm that comes to those who are heedless of others and careless of their own affairs. Like Frost, O'Connor was alert to the dangers of existence. Although she trusted in God's mercy, she was keenly aware of the countless ways in which human beings can be hurt. In such a world, it was imperative that one live carefully and practice charity toward others. As O'Connor wrote to Betty Hester, the correspondent identified only as "A" in *The Habit of Being*, "Every opportunity for performing any kind of charity is something to be snatched at" (*Habit* 214).

Still, Edmunds is correct in half of her argument: the racist and sexist aspects of the South and of the world as a whole are rejected by O'Connor, but so much should be obvious to anyone who considers O'Connor's profoundly orthodox Christian vision. The other side of Edmunds' argument, that as a consequence of her awareness of suffering, O'Connor devotes her art to advancing a radical social agenda, is utterly mistaken. The implication of suffering, as O'Connor understands it, is not that we should devote our lives exclusively or even predominantly to ending its existence in the world—a pointless and frustrating task, because to do so we must overlook the fact that suffering will always exist—but that because of its existence, we must turn to the comfort of a promise of reunion with Christ at the end of time. If, as Edmunds would have it, we were able to achieve a world in which all forms of adversity have been eliminated, there would be no point in the promise of redemption. Christ would be coming to redeem a world that was already redeemed.

In fact, at no point in her fiction does O'Connor suggest the possibility of such a perfectibility of the immanent world, and yet Edmunds is not by any means the only critic to suggest that O'Connor was primarily motivated by social issues of race or gender. David Havird, for example, focuses on the imagery of rape in three of O'Connor's stories ("Greenleaf," "Revelation," and "Good Country People") to reveal the violence and sexual humiliation that he believes is connected with patriarchal religion. According to Havird, "it is [O'Connor's] strategy…to knock these proud female characters down a notch…by forcing upon them, in a sexually humiliating and often violent way, the humbling knowledge that they are after all women" (15). Havird's speculation is that, given the patriarchal culture in which she writes and practices her faith, O'Connor is controlled by a sense of guilt connected with her role as a female who takes on the "male" role of authorship: "In these displaced enactments of self-flagellation, the monstrous female characters become scapegoats for Flannery O'Connor, whose sin of authorship is greater even than their own prideful rejection of woman's conventional role as angel of the house" (25).

Needless to say, I find this interpretation highly implausible. Certainly, Havird is correct in stressing that O'Connor addresses the sin of pride in the characters of Mrs. May, Joy/Hulga Hopewell, and Ruby Turpin, but his interpretation takes into account neither the destructiveness of their pride—a condition that is much in need of repair—nor the essentially comic resolution of each of the stories. Nor does Havird's reading clearly distinguish between the linguistic differences in sexual connotation in the three stories. The idea of a figurative rape is appropriate to "Good Country People" but not to "Greenleaf" nor to "Revelation," in both of which the bridegroom may be said to come as a lover, not as a rapist. In any event, the attempt to reduce O'Connor's complex imaginative prose to the reductive terms of human sexuality is an exercise in materialist interpretation that seems completely inappropriate in O'Connor's case. In none of the three stories, when read as a whole, is the female character demeaned or subjugated: all of the stories conclude with the suggestion of an opening of a life-affirming admission of need and of an acceptance of Christ's redemptive love.

Havird attempts to proceed from the premise that the repressiveness of O'Connor's existence within a patriarchal culture—presumably any culture influenced by Christian or even Western thinking—led to a condition of rage that found expression in her "vindictive" attacks on women. An important aspect of this life, of course, was the fact that O'Connor never married, and recent critics and biographers have attempted, none too subtly, to link the idea of her spinsterhood with the harsh orthodoxy of her imagination. Her biographer, Jean W. Cash, contends that, "even before the onset of her illness, [O'Connor] considered fashion or dating unimportant and found the idea of marriage shocking." Cash endeavors to anchor this judgment in feminist theory by stating that O'Connor "refused to accept the 1940s notion of southern womanhood with its roots in the pre-Civil War South" (xvi). Although Cash provides details of the close friendship between O'Connor and Robie Macauley, who claimed to have dated O'Connor while they were graduate students at the University of Iowa, and though Sally Fitzgerald, O'Connor's longtime friend, "believed that the relationship was serious from O'Connor's point of view, that she fell in love with Macauley and was deeply hurt when her love for him remained unrequited" (Cash 99), Cash characterizes the possibility of the existence of a romantic relationship as "questionable," although she hedges on this point later, quoting passages from O'Connor's letters that suggest a different story.

If we are to credit her statements to Betty Hester, O'Connor had, indeed, experienced romantic feelings on numerous occasions, and she was not in any sense a woman who "disliked" men, as Cash implies. In a letter to Hester on 24 August 1956, O'Connor discussed the character of Hulga in "Good Country People," a character that she said "is like me." Hester had assumed that Hulga, the character who resembled O'Connor, had never experienced romantic love, but O'Connor repeatedly insisted that she was wrong. O'Connor wrote that in the story "it is not said that she has never loved anybody, only that she's never been kissed by anybody—a very different thing." O'Connor then elaborated concerning her own feelings: "That my stories scream to you that I have never consented to be in love with anybody is merely to prove that they are screaming an historical inaccuracy. I have God help me consented to this frequently" (*Habit* 170–71).

In a previous letter to Hester, O'Connor, while speaking of the fact that her father wrote only "speeches and local political stuff," stated that: "Needing people badly and not getting them may turn you in a creative direction, provided you have the other requirements. He needed the people and got them...I wanted them and didn't" (*Habit* 169). Again, on 25 November 1955, O'Connor wrote to Hester that though "he-and-she" relations might seem to be somewhat absent in her writing, this was not because she felt that romance was not virtuous: just the opposite, more than a matter of virtue, human love must be identified with the sacred. Almost apologetically, O'Connor told Hester that "my upbringing has smacked a little of Jansenism even if my convictions do not" (*Habit* 117). Perhaps it was her degree of seriousness as a young woman, a student, and then an artist and the circumstance of her illness, which soon reduced her to bedridden periods and to crutches, that made it unlikely that O'Connor would ever marry, but this does not imply, as Cash appears to do, that O'Connor at some early point in her life decided to shun romance for art and afterward put her emotions under lock and key. The sense that she expresses in her stories is quite a conventional desire for a traditional home life and a highly traditional yearning for male companionship, security, and authority.

What the sociohistorical interpretation overlooks in its effort to find a discrete motive of race, gender, or class behind O'Connor's fiction is the greater tradition of ethical thought in which she is writing. O'Connor shows little interest in the partisan struggles that would transform American society, at least superficially, during the 1950s and 1960s. While she supported social justice, her vision was focused on a broader and more ancient philosophical and religious tradition that teaches self-restraint, charity, and concern for the common good as principal virtues. Joy/Hulga and Ruby Turpin are sinful characters, not because they are somehow sacrificed to O'Connor's resentment of her own supposed limitations as a woman but because they have become cynical and complacent in a way that is not uniquely modern, though it may be characteristic of the period since the Renaissance that one refers to as modernity: they believe that they "see through" existence, in effect that they see better than does their Creator. Significantly, O'Connor's male protagonists, including Haze Motes, suffer from precisely the same limitations.

In the history of Western thought, as Maritain points out, it was the philosophy of Machiavelli that best embodied this modern temptation, one that is rooted in the larger sin of human pride. As Maritain writes, "Machiavelli belongs to that series of minds...which all through modern times have endeavored to unmask the human being" ("Machiavellianism" 294). This "unmasking" at the heart of Machiavelli's political realism turns a skeptical eye on all claims of idealism or higher principles: in place of the Christian ideal of self-sacrifice, it justifies selfishness and ambition as it condones ruthlessness and violence in the service of political realism. After Machiavelli, it became ever more difficult to affirm the ideals of Christianity in the context of practical affairs, since Machiavelli's "crude empiricism cancels for him the image of God in man" (Maritain, "Machiavellianism" 295). It was precisely this normalization of selfishness that Faulkner had in mind in his Nobel acceptance speech, in which, urging future writers to return to the "old universal truths," he characterized modernity as a "curse" under which one "writes not of love but of lust, of defeats in which nobody loses anything of value, of victories without hope and, worst of all, without pity or compassion" ("Address" 724).

Within the secular tradition of Machiavellianism, the religious structure of O'Connor's fiction is dismissed, and her complex imagery is reduced to either sociohistorical or Freudian terms. Such a reading, for example, tends to interpret the repetitive use of the color yellow in *Wise Blood*, including the image of Slades' son at the used car lot, the "dried yellow color" (*Collected Works* 56) of the mummy that Enoch Emery steals from the museum, and other "mixed-color" images, in racial terms. This reductive reading ignores the fact that it is not merely human beings who are depicted as yellow but also the objective world. It is not only skin color in *Wise Blood* that is yellow but the city as a whole, a world that is irretrievably fallen. The grotesque connotation of the color yellow implies the condition in which all human beings are merged in the sense that they are "yellowed" by sin, not as a result of racial mixing but as a result of the rejection of grace that O'Connor associates with the materialistic lifestyle of urban industrial society. In fact, the yellowing of the world that Haze discovers in Taulkinham extends well beyond the matter of race to the sky, the earth, and the color of houses.

Similarly, the character of the Pullman porter, "a thick-figured man with a round yellow bald head" whom Haze takes to be "a Parrum nigger from Eastrod" (*Collected Works* 5), is more significant in terms of the secular myth than in racial terms. While Edmunds finds that the porter suggests the upward social mobility and empowerment—and thus materialist salvation—of African Americans during the 1940s and 1950s, in reality, he functions in the structure of the novel as the agent of Haze's initiation to the pitiless and friendless society of modern urban America. In terms of the agrarian mythology that informs O'Connor's thinking, the fact that he hails from Chicago rather than the rural South helps to explain his air of unfeeling arrogance. He projects not a white point of light, an image that would suggest the star over Bethlehem associated with the Annunciation, but a more ambiguous "white shape in the darkness" (*Collected Works* 14). It is doubtful that the porter is to be mistaken for a messianic double of Christ, given his dismissive rejection of Haze's fear at the idea of being closed up in a Pullman berth. When Haze calls on Christ for relief, the porter "in a sour triumphant voice" proclaims that "Jesus been a long time gone" (*Collected Works* 14).

Likewise, Edmunds' suggestion that the consumer and service industries, for which all of the women in the novel work and which seem to comprise the predominant economy of Taulkinham, represent a means of liberation is at odds with O'Connor's vision. Consumer culture is indeed an important target of O'Connor's critique in *Wise Blood*, but the predominant sense that attaches to consumer culture is one of futility and waste: it is by no means a liberation, but a false siren song, leading the people of the city away from the true salvation that comes from relinquishment of the motive of vanity that attaches itself to acquisition. The activities of consumerism that O'Connor describes are characterized by their qualities of cheapness, transitoriness, and degradation. Participation in such a culture can hardly be termed liberating for any human being but particularly not for women. The prostitute, Leona Watts, who might be said to work as a "wage-earner" in a service industry, can hardly be imagined to have anything but a base and degrading existence. She is not a woman who has been liberated from patriarchy by means of her wage-earning outside the home but one who is doomed by the corruption of the world. The point of the maternal imagery attached to her is to suggest her total loss of the meaningful life that she might have enjoyed within a family. Now all that is left to her is the sad travesty of the maternal role.

The false idol of consumerism is one aspect of the urban secular culture to which Haze is drawn as a result of his rebellion against and dissatisfaction with the seemingly confined quality of his inherited religious culture. One of the most horrifying scenes in *Wise Blood* is that in which Haze is initially converted to agnosticism. In this intensely dramatic scene, O'Connor is able to embody in vivid detail the appeal of agnosticism based on its undemanding ethos of indifference and alienation. Haze's Army buddies, young ruffians who are untroubled by spiritual questions, are out to enjoy the pleasures of physical existence that from Haze's perspective are identified as "evil": drinking, gambling, and whoring. Even as he resists these temptations, Haze sets out on a course that is more dangerous. At the point in the novel at which he refuses to accompany his fellow recruits to the brothel, he saw "the opportunity to get rid of [his soul] and to be converted to nothing instead of to evil" (*Collected Works* 12). Haze is prescient in his choice of sin: as with most pseudo-sophisticated moderns, it is not old-fashioned evil that tempts Haze but the powerful allure of escapism. It is not the sinful choice of evil over good that he seeks but the possibility of a world without good or evil.

Haze's character does, of course, contain evil, but it is important to define its nature precisely. Among others, Richard Giannone has attempted to link Haze's "nihilism" with contemporary events, particularly with World War II in which he had fought and suffered a severe wound, yet Giannone overestimates the impact of world events on *Wise Blood*, a novel that takes place in a nearly allegorical setting and in which the protagonist's development centers on a turning away from historical reality. While O'Connor would certainly have viewed the war and the Holocaust, along with the dislocation that followed, as confirmation of the universal alienation of earthly existence, she would have recognized that, though the scale of suffering in the modern period was immense, the essential nature of humanity did not change during the period. That is to say, while the rise of technology and the reach of science had enabled a greater potential for human evil, the global carnage of World War II was not a unique event in history. What is increasingly common in modern history, according to O'Connor, is the tendency of modern man to dismiss the importance of religious experience altogether. While the evil of the recent global conflict was immense, it was the disengagement of her contemporaries, not so much their involvement in active forms of evil, that troubled O'Connor. It is remarkable that not once in the six hundred pages of her published letters does the name Adolf Hitler appear, and that Mussolini, who is mentioned once, is referred to as merely "a gangster" (*Habit* 347). Admittedly, references to the Holocaust become an important part of the imaginative structure of "The Displaced Person," "The Enduring Chill," "Revelation," and other stories, and yet even in these instances there is a tendency to comprehend discrete historical events as part of a universal pattern of meaning.

As O'Connor made clear in essays such as "The Fiction Writer and His Country," within postwar society the movement towards agnosticism was the greatest threat to Christian society. Unwilling to admit his own evil, Haze practices a travesty of religious belief, and in this way, he resembles a large segment of the American population that wishes to discard traditional Christian dogma but retain a sense of itself as innately good. Although Haze shares this desire to escape the spiritual obligations entailed in participation in a particular tradition of inherited belief, he resists this temptation because of the spiritual knowledge or instinct deep within him, an unappeasable yearning for truth that he appears to have inherited from his mother, and that, along with his mother's eyeglasses, lends a peculiarly concentrated expression to his face. Although Haze will eventually discard his mother's eyeglasses in his pursuit of a vision of a more inward and hopeful nature, there is little doubt that the legacy of her spiritual temper and dissatisfaction with the immanent world is what sets him on his quest.

Once he arrives in the city of Taulkinham, Haze finds that his residual faith is sorely tested by the overwhelmingly secular quality of the city. This urban secularism is perfectly embodied in a scene in which a street salesman attempts to hawk potato peelers that he claims will bring happiness and completion to an existence that, in reality, is as dull and purposeless as peeling potatoes. The salesman's claim that anyone who purchases a potato peeler "will never forget it" is, on its face, utterly ludicrous for the obvious reason that a small, insignificant mechanical contraption cannot supply any lasting meaning to existence, and yet the salesman's claims for the efficacy of the peeler points toward Haze's own claims of the satisfaction to be found in a well-built automobile. If the possession of an automobile is all that is necessary to bring about happiness, where can one draw the line? Why not a potato peeler? The Essex automobile that Haze later purchases is so bizarrely unsatisfactory as to be almost endearing. Its shabby appearance, mechanical unreliability, and overall lack of respectability make it a perfect embodiment of the cheapness and futility of consumer culture as an alternative to the genuine satisfactions of the life of contemplation. As one who only learned to drive late in life and then only out of necessity, O'Connor was peculiarly alert to the metaphorical implications of the automobile and to its significance within postwar American culture. Like everything sold within consumer culture, Haze's Essex is a disposable object that quickly loses its value and that eventually fails to function at all. In her wonderful descriptions of the automobile's insufficiency, O'Connor humorously belittles the pretensions of the mechanical age. The car horn, which "made it sound like goats laughed cut off with a buzz saw" (*Collected Works* 91), is merely one example.

It is not the urban industrial culture and its secular values, including prominently its belief in self-gratification as the goal of existence, but the heartland values of small-town and rural America that O'Connor celebrated. The small-town, middle-class society into which she was born and in which she lived nearly all of her life was a provincial one, but within this society she arrived at a positive acceptance of her so-called limitations, indeed even a heroic embrace of them. Her acceptance of what she regarded as the limited range of her talent was a necessary step toward happiness, leading as it did to self-acceptance and an appropriate degree of satisfaction in her achievement. In her everyday life, she practiced a humble appreciation of the small-town society of Milledgeville, as well as an association with church leaders who were obviously provincial, and of life on a working farm on which her mother struggled to make a living for the family, and an acceptance of what she herself was, including her illness and the limited range of her life that resulted from it. The impact of her illness, as she said, was not something that should be exaggerated. All human beings live with limitations of uncertainty and fear, and life is never completely satisfying. What was remarkable about O'Connor was her determination to find meaning and beauty in the world as it was and not to try to remake the world into something else. This helps to explain the constant humor of O'Connor's writing, for this humor is simply the record of O'Connor's fondness for the life she was given. Furthermore, the humor that she practiced can only emanate from a person who is honest about who she is and forthright about her identity. O'Connor's humor reflects a rightful pride in where she comes from and what she is rather than embarrassment at her past or a desire for sweeping social change.

Although many critics have dealt with O'Connor's use of southern "manners" in her fiction, few have recognized the depth of this loyalty to her region, nor has the broader significance of this loyalty been generally understood. The importance of a person's relation to a local culture—in her case variously defined as the South, middle Georgia, or Milledgeville—is stressed repeatedly in O'Connor's essays and letters, and it is implicit in her fiction. Living within a local culture demanded that one publicly acknowledge that culture's values, even if one privately disagreed with certain aspects of them. When O'Connor's friend, Maryat Lee, suggested that she entertain James Baldwin at Andalusia, O'Connor refused, noting that "I observe the traditions of the society I feed on" (*Habit* 329). There were, of course, practical reasons for this position: in the Deep South in 1959, for two white women to welcome a black male as a guest in their home would have involved great difficulties. O'Connor had to consider not only her own position but also that of her mother, and her mother was even more dependent upon the local society of Milledgeville than was O'Connor. Yet, even if one discounts the practical barriers, O'Connor might not have been willing to host a writer like Baldwin, whose work, as she came to know it later, was offensive to her because of its arrogant "pontificating" (*Habit* 580). It was not that O'Connor disliked Baldwin because he was black or because she considered him unequal on racial grounds. Her dislike of this prominent African American writer was not based on the local tradition of racial superiority, and yet it was related to O'Connor's embrace of local tradition in another, more subtle, respect. As a writer and as a human being, Baldwin was objectionable because of his arrogance, and his arrogance was embodied primarily in the fact that his values transcended the constraints of all particularized traditions and systems of value. In other words, O'Connor's disregard for Baldwin had less to do with southern attitudes toward race in their stereotypical form but did have to do with race, class, gender, region, religion, and all other aspects of inherited culture of the sort that Baldwin's universalizing perspective denied. Even if Baldwin had visited O'Connor in Milledgeville, it is difficult to imagine that they would have had anything to say to one another, so completely opposite were their views and beliefs.

The disinclination to host James Baldwin was merely one example of a broader pattern of social conservatism. Although O'Connor resided in the Deep South in the years of the civil rights movement, she did not contribute to that movement. While she credited the efforts of Martin Luther King, she strongly mistrusted the efforts of more radical leaders who came to the fore in the 1960s, and she was vocal in her opposition. The very idea of integration must have seemed puzzling to one who already lived on a daily basis in close contact with black farm workers. O'Connor was not in any sense a racist, but she did not go out of her way to mix socially with other races. At the time when she was living in Milledgeville, there would have been few if any non-whites with whom she could have discussed the matters closest to her heart: her theological interests, her interest in contemporary writing, and her interest in philosophy. There were certainly few *whites* with whom she could discuss these matters, and as a consequence O'Connor was regarded by most of her fellow townspeople as distinctly eccentric. Her active correspondence with writers and intellectuals outside Milledgeville compensated to some degree for this lack.

Perhaps a more important reason why O'Connor made no effort to court the company of minorities, however, can be traced to the fact that she refused to categorize any group as such. She refused to speak of "the poor, because I don't like to distinguish them," she wrote to Betty Hester. "Everybody, as far as I am concerned, is the Poor" (*Habit* 103). She was also very far from being a feminist. Indeed, she viewed all forms of social change with skepticism, a point that goes to the heart of her sensibility. Change for its own sake is harmful in the sense that it always involves a wrenching adjustment for those whom it affects. O'Connor viewed the rapidly changing society of the late 1950s and early 1960s with concern, and she was prescient enough to look ahead to the turbulence and moral chaos that would transpire after her death in 1964. O'Connor embraced the four cardinal virtues that have been recognized for thousands of years in Christian tradition: prudence, justice, fortitude, and temperance, and, to a large extent, these are values that suggest a resistance to change rather than advocacy of social experimentation.

Indeed, *Wise Blood* is a brilliant and often humorous polemic directed not only against the widespread indifference and apathy that O'Connor detects in the postwar culture but also against its heedless willingness to discard such a valuable tradition of beliefs. In Haze's preaching of the Church Without Christ, O'Connor exposes the damage of a culture that questions all inherited traditions and yet believes itself capable of fashioning a framework of belief out of thin air. Haze's conception of a Church Without Christ perfectly reflects the postwar temper, since what he offers his followers is a travesty of traditional belief in which the individual retains a sense of self-directed moral order yet finds himself free of all traditional obligations. This is precisely what Haze intends by his assertion that "there are all kinds of truth, your truth and somebody else's, but behind all of them, there's only one truth and that is that there's no truth" (*Collected Works* 93). Such a position, however, opens the door to any number of fraudulent belief systems, from the blatant quackery of con artists such as Onnie Jay Holy to the more insidious religious cults that would appear with increasing frequently in the decades following O'Connor's death.

The most powerful rival to Christianity during O'Connor's lifetime, however, was represented by Marxism, a cult of materialism that explicitly asserted its intention to supersede traditional forms of religion. Surprisingly few critics have considered the significance of O'Connor's writing in relation to the Cold War, and of those who do, they have, for whatever reason, failed to see just how adamantly she opposed Marxism in every form. Jon Lance Bacon's *Flannery O'Connor and the Cold War Culture* presents the case for reading O'Connor as a radical critic of American culture and of American foreign policy during the Cold War era. Unfortunately, the evidence suggests that quite the opposite was the case. O'Connor was not alienated from middle-class America, though she was repelled by its increasing materialism and spiritual indifference, and she was never an ideological opponent of capitalism. What Bacon mistakes for a sociohistorical critique was, in fact, a religious commitment that necessarily diminished the importance of the immanent world but did not dismiss its value *as* immanent world.

Lest anyone argue that this code of virtues has simply been rearticulated in more relevant terms by Hegel, Marx, and other materialist thinkers, Jacques Maritain makes it clear that modern materialism, while perhaps motivated initially by the Christian virtue of charity, is actually a grotesque inversion and travesty of Christianity. Communism preaches its own religion, that of atheism, that stands in unswerving opposition to Christian belief. Not only was it Maritain's view that Marxism was not an acceptable substitute for Christianity, it was his belief that communism represented a danger far greater than the political or economic challenge that it posed to the West. O'Connor viewed the struggle in precisely the same terms, writing to Ted Spivey that "Communism is a religion of the state, committed to the extinction of the Church" (*Habit* 347). Once her reputation was established and her works began to be translated, O'Connor informed her agent Elizabeth McKee "that she didn't want her work published in 'Russian-occupied' countries because she feared that they might use it to promote 'anti-American propaganda'" (Cash 120). In this response she was aligned with conservatives such as Maritain rather than with radical critics of American Cold War politics such as Mary McCarthy.

Haze Motes would seem to be a candidate for just the sort of intellectual pride that O'Connor detected in so many of her contemporaries, including McCarthy: a defiance of divine will and an attraction to power that, Richard Giannone points out, was viewed as "demonic" within the eremitic tradition of Christianity (50). Haze is certainly possessed by the demons of rebellion and pride, but the problem, or good fortune, for Haze in this respect is that he is not convinced by his own proofs of relativism and free will. In fact, his strenuous effort to refute the need for an ultimum outside natural existence and beyond the control of human reason only leads him toward the opposite conclusion. Impelled by an inner hunger for final truths, Haze is driven to ferret out all of the implications of the troubling and contradictory position that he has embraced. Unlike the postwar generation as a whole, which simply wishes to be left alone with the senseless and insufficient travesty of spiritual life that it has accepted, Haze, despite his claim that there is no truth, is relentlessly tracking down the gaps in his own philosophy and moving toward a clearer understanding of the necessity for origins. This becomes apparent in what follows his assertion that no objective truth exists: if no truth exists, then as Haze himself makes clear, "nothing outside you can give you any place" (*Collected Works* 93).

In this instinctive focus on the rootless condition of modern life, Haze stresses the central quality of postmodern existence, a quality that is actually celebrated rather than lamented by such critics as Gabriel Josipovici. In his 1999 book *On Trust*, Gabriel Josipovici argues that "migration, not rootedness, is our promised land," a place of a sort in which one can "cease to be a stranger" to oneself (48). In contrast to Josipovici's confident assertion in the virtues of uncertainty, insecurity, and disorder, O'Connor's protagonist in *Wise Blood* is constantly running up against the damaging consequences of just such forms of negation. When he purchases the beat-up Essex automobile for forty dollars, Haze enters a new stage of spiritual rebellion, at once more hopeful and more desperate than what preceded it. Haze intends the automobile to be not only a physical shelter but a spiritual temple that will take the place of his yearning for completion and wholeness. His protestation that the worthless machine is better than other vehicles because it was not built by blacks, immigrants, or one-armed men only masks his growing knowledge that there exists no real earthly home for anyone, least of all for prophets like himself. In fact, the effect of his acquisition is to carry him further into the world of experience in which his "wise blood" encounters greater confirmation of his inherited sense of the chaos and suffering that are an inevitable part of life. When he is finally rid of the automobile, he is free to move beyond the fantasized shelter that it provides and onto the next stage in his spiritual development.

With an extraordinary foresight and vision, O'Connor anticipated the philosophical challenge of postmodernism, and in her novels and stories she offered a savage refutation of the fraudulent secular culture that would arise in the half-century after the publication of *Wise Blood*. Haze himself, of course, comes to understand the fraudulence of this culture and the fact of his own participation in it. This is made clear in the scene in which he confronts his own double, a look-alike preacher named Solace Layfield dressed exactly like Haze. The lie that Haze finds objectionable in Solace's mimicry of his own preaching is the very fact that Solace, beneath the surface of his mimicry of fraudulence, is true, while Haze, in his continued rejection of the truth, remains for the time being false. Even though Haze forces Solace to unmask by removing the hat and suit that mimic his own, and even after he has eliminated his rival by running over him with his car, Haze is unable to remove these contradictions from his mind. In fact, Solace's dying words, which take the form of a confession in which he calls on Jesus for rescue, point the narrative by a clear inner logic toward the scene in which Haze's car is destroyed by a patrolman who finds Haze instinctually repugnant and in which Haze, in the climax of the narrative, blinds himself.

Haze's blinding of himself is the point at which the theme of vision is clarified and resolved. While the blinding separates Haze from the world of social experience—not because it renders him sightless but because its nature permanently marks Haze as one who stands in opposition to the fraudulence of society—it also comprises the commencement of his serious engagement with existence following a lifetime of futile attempts to evade reality. After the blinding, Haze's eyes are no longer focused on the muddled corruption of the immanent world; instead, freed from the distraction of race, gender, class, and other matters of social identity, he is able to conceive his place in the context of a divine telos. The sinful world in which human suffering will always exist is transfigured into a world that is to be redeemed. Significantly, the force of social conflict that historicist critics wish to address are ameliorated following this transfiguration. At the end of the novel, Haze relinquishes all interest in money and practical affairs, a "current of renunciation" that, as Giannone puts it, "flows as an antidote to the history of sin and violence" out of which Haze emerges (62). The paradox is that, with this renunciation of the world of experience, Haze gains an unprecedented empathy toward other human beings. The harsh, defensive mask slips away, and beneath it is revealed a person capable of love for God and for his fellow man. His relationship to his landlady is transformed, and there is even a sense of Christ-like forgiveness for the callous policemen who beat him and then carry him "home" to Mrs. Flood's lodging.

It is the very nature of this extreme act of blinding, an intentional abnegation of sensory satisfaction of the sort that sets Haze against the dominant hedonistic values of postwar American culture, that suggests the possibility of his gaining a following. Even before his deliberate act of self-blinding, of course, Haze had gained disciples in the persons of Sabbath Lily Hawks and Enoch Emery, although both of them, for their own reasons, had misunderstood Haze's mission. For her part, Sabbath Lily was attracted to the intensity of Haze's gaze, but she misinterpreted this intensity as lustful rather than religious in nature. She appears to be seeking a romantic partner who resembles her father, a fraudulent preacher who has sired a "bastard" daughter, Sabbath Lily herself, and who has backed down on his promise to blind himself in front of his congregation. When Sabbath Lily discovers that Haze is serious in all the ways that her father is not, she is appalled.

The lonely Enoch pursues Haze as a potential ally in the unfriendly city, but he is, as Margaret Earley Whitt points out, intended mainly as a "foil" to Haze. Enoch's search for meaning and human communion takes the form of a travesty of genuine religion, a senseless round of repeated "meaningless acts of ritual" (Whitt 20). Because his own experience is ruled by a reflexive need to assuage his emotional emptiness, Enoch looks hopefully to any source of instruction, especially that emanating from such a willful and self-assured figure as Haze. Enoch's ritualistic existence at the city park and zoo where he works, a daily round of sterile activities that includes poolside voyeurism, animal harassment, and obsession with a museum mummy, is evidence of a hopelessly negative condition before the arrival of Haze. Like the museum mummy, Enoch himself is a spiritually dried-up soul, one who lives in an attic residence with "a mummified look and feel" (*Collected Works* 73).

The reason for Enoch's failure is of crucial importance. Enoch is aware that something is missing in his life—to this extent he possesses "wise blood" like Haze—but he lacks the *wiser* blood to pursue knowledge in any place other than in the material world, an approach that results in a travesty of faith and in the unclean acts of voyeurism, harassment, and insult that he reflexively commits. Clearly, his search for meaning only carries him further into the fraudulent world of unbelief, and, in this respect, Enoch is a particularly important and representative character within O'Connor's canon, a figure who would reappear many times in various guises. The ease with which O'Connor created Enoch's character, according to her own testimony, can be explained by the fact that the sort of hapless, bewildered secularist whose every impulse towards spirituality carries him a step further away from spiritual understanding is one of O'Connor's enduring concerns. Enoch, the pitiful hangdog character who inspires so much of our contempt, is, perhaps, the most representative of O'Connor's figures and one that is the norm in modern existence. He is the human being who dutifully works his job, grudgingly putting in the extra fifteen minutes a day, and then after work seeks satisfaction and meaning in life through self-gratification or through shifting and fraudulent forms of belief. As Whitt points out, the mummy that Enoch presents to Haze Motes as a culminating act of their joint endeavor (as Enoch sees it) perfectly represents the "new jesus" that Haze himself has preached, but that he now finds unsatisfactory. As Whitt writes, Haze understands that what he has called for is "not what his church needs and not what he needs or believes" (22). When he throws the mummy against the wall and finds that it is bloodless inside, his suspicions of the fraudulence of Enoch's gift and of his own former preaching are confirmed.

The overwhelming sense in *Wise Blood* is of a world of nonbeing populated by creatures such as Enoch or Sabbath Lily who subsist at a bestial or mechanical level. In this world, the sort of spiritual impulses that still exist find expression in all sorts of confused ways. Having lost all sense of their place within an inherited religious or cultural tradition, the inhabitants of this world exhibit no knowledge of the way in which myth operates within human existence. Their every impulse comprises a naive travesty of true culture and belief, and their struggles toward a kind of happiness are fruitless as a result of their total ignorance of the way in which life needs to be ordered and informed by faith. Within this environment, morality is utterly disregarded. It is a world populated by the likes of Leora Watts, a prostitute who, as she says, does not care whether her customers are respectable or not. It is populated by those who seek love as a commodity, or by those like Sabbath Lily, whose search for love takes the form of a perverse inversion of true love. In contrast with all of these characters, Haze retains a sense of the needfulness of this world. His wise blood makes it possible for him to see this immanent world for what it is, and it allows him to retain the sort of open mind that will eventually lead to a receptiveness towards grace.

Precisely because of the effect of grace on his personality, Haze gains an even more ardent follower than Sabbath Lily or Enoch Emery in the person of his landlady, Mrs. Flood. In a perceptive reading, Giannone points out that she is a far more complex character than many critics recognize. As Giannone insists, Mrs. Flood has essentially given up on the spiritual journey that she intuitively glimpses and values, yet, with the repeated and ever more extreme acts of self-humbling that Haze performs, Mrs. Flood begins to be troubled by "the thought that there might be something valuable hidden near her, something she couldn't see" (*Collected Works* 120). While Mrs. Flood does not yet comprehend the spiritual nature of this treasure, she becomes more and more devoted to Haze, even as she discovers further acts of self-laceration, to the point that, as Giannone suggests, when she holds the deceased Haze's hand to her heart, this act comprises "the only time in *Wise Blood* when two characters touch without intending to control or harm the other person" (63). It is these facts that force Mrs. Flood to the admission that the physical world is an "empty place" and that presumably point toward the deepening of her spiritual understanding. At the end of the novel, Mrs. Flood's expression, staring at the corpse of Haze Motes and appearing to see the beginning of something she cannot fully comprehend, provides us with a clue to the reception of Haze's true ministry. As Giannone observes, "At heart, Mrs. Flood is benevolent and akin to Motes. Both are solitaries; both struggle against desolation and ruin" (34).

Still, Haze has discovered a healing communion with God that has not yet been glimpsed by his landlady. In a profound analysis of the difference between individuality and personality, one that would have been known to O'Connor either directly from the 1947 essay "The Individual and the Person" or from its restatement elsewhere in his writing, Jacques Maritain describes the seeking of the human personality for "knowledge and love" outside of itself, "a dialogue in which souls really communicate." As a result of this dependence upon others who, because of their inherent human weaknesses, are necessarily insufficient to a perfect fulfillment of these needs, personality "seems to be bound to the experience of affliction." Beyond the knowledge and love of this world, needs that no human being ever puts aside, "the person has a direct relation with the absolute, and only in the absolute is he able to have his full sufficiency" ("Individual" 8).

From a very early age, O'Connor seems to have understood the intricate relationship of person to world and to the absolute that Maritain theorized. One of the implications of this understanding of the necessary limitation of even the most valued relationship to others is the importance of a careful and caring regard for life, a protecting and conserving that is at the core of O'Connor's writing. In practical terms, this attitude suggested caution in regard to the fundamental institutions and relationships of the private life. In terms of her attitude toward marriage and the family, O'Connor was not a champion of the changes that she foresaw taking place. In a great number of her stories, O'Connor portrays families in which a father figure is lacking and in which relations of parents and children are painfully alienated. In these portraits of broken families, O'Connor registers the pain that she feels as a conservative regarding the effects of change on the family. In relation to these portraits of harassed and working women, of what we would today call "single mothers," of absent or indifferent fathers, and of their often hopeless children, O'Connor implicitly contrasts the ideal of a family in which parents and children lead purposeful and selfless lives.

Despite the efforts of many academics to make O'Connor into a closeted champion of civil rights or a frustrated feminist, or, in the very different case of Richard Giannone, into a "postdogmatic" novelist whose work focuses on a "renunciation" of the world that "transcends any political ideology" (64), the fact is that O'Connor was a deeply religious and socially conservative person who did not withhold her political and social opinions from her art; although these opinions were in no way the central focus of her life or art, they were nonetheless an inevitable part of living in the experiential world. It is not surprising that in a letter from early 1964 she wrote, upside down in capital letters at the bottom of the letter as if in an intentionally transparent secret code, VOTE FOR GOLDWATER. If at this point in her life O'Connor was a Goldwater conservative, she had always been a social conservative, a fact that should be apparent from her position during the Agnes Smedley affair at Yadoo in 1949. O'Connor was one of only four residents in the Yadoo artists' colony (along with Robert Lowell, Elizabeth Hardwick, and Edward Maisel) who insisted on the resignation of the colony's director, Elizabeth Ames, largely on the basis of her deferential treatment of Agnes Smedley, a resident with communist associations. Within a month, the Yadoo board received a petition signed by forty-four prominent writers, including Alfred Kazin, Katherine Anne Porter, and John Cheever, in support of Ames. With Lowell, Hardwick, and Maisel, O'Connor quit Yadoo in protest. She moved first to New York City and then to Ridgefield, Connecticut, where she lived with Robert and Sally Fitzgerald and their family.

The Yadoo scandal gave O'Connor an early taste of just how treacherous literary politics could be, and it must also have given her a sense of how isolated and unpopular her position as a social conservative and an orthodox

Catholic would be later in her life. During her brief residence in New York City during the spring and summer of 1949, O'Connor met and dealt with a number of critics, intellectuals, and professional literati, including Mary McCarthy, a prominent liberal author whom O'Connor derided as an agnostic, a pretentious intellectual, and a poor writer. Conversely, O'Connor described the pleasure—though an awkward one on both their parts—of her meeting with prominent conservative intellectual Russell Kirk, who was just then launching *The Conservative Review*. Based on her knowledge of Kirk, whose *The Conservative Mind* she had read and "admired" and whose *Beyond the Dreams of Avarice* she was later to review, O'Connor said that the new conservative journal "should be very good" (*Habit* 112).

O'Connor's conservative temperament produced an art that was highly original in its grasp of the damage done by a radical dismissal of tradition and a heedless desire for social innovation. Much of her originality can be traced to her courage in defending her fundamental beliefs: the belief in the distinction between good and evil, the belief in salvation and divine grace, and the belief in the virtues of renunciation and acceptance. O'Connor's own temperament was a reflection and product of these deep-seated beliefs: she was a modest person who did not boast of her virtues, but she did often use the word "purity" in connection with her own life and art, and, paradoxically, it was perhaps the purity of her soul that made it possible for O'Connor to employ fictional images that were considered by her contemporaries to be shocking productions, particularly for a southern middle-class woman of her generation. What is truly disturbing about the world that O'Connor summons up, however, is not propensity for greed, lust, or violence in her characters but the pervasiveness of indifference. Indeed, the affliction of a character such as Haze Motes, a haunted soul who finds himself comfortless in the modern urban wasteland, opens the door to redemptive salvation. As Maritain wrote in *The Person and the Common Good*, "personality in man seems to be bound to the experience of affliction" (32). This is because of the fact that, though human personality by its very nature seeks a fulfilling "dialogue" with others, it finds its most perfect dialogue with the absolute, not with other human beings. "Its spiritual homeland is the whole universe of the absolute and of those indefectible goods which are as the pathways to the absolute Whole which transcends the world" (32). *Wise Blood*, like O'Connor's other fictional works, is not merely a vision of a broken world: it is her guide into the spiritual homeland by way of affliction and an uncompromising demand for truth.

7

Redemption of Ordinary Delight: Mary Hood's Familiar Heat

Mary Hood's fictional world is a fearful place. It is a place where all of the tragedies and ills of life derive from sources ordinary enough but that seem to strike with unusual intensity and frequency. It is a world in which one grasps what joy one can from life knowing that any such pleasure is short-lived. It is a place where human relations are seemingly unpredictable and accidental, and perhaps, most importantly, it is an unjust place in which kindnesses are not reciprocated, responsibilities are not always met, and fidelity is the exception rather than the rule. Given the moral anarchy that Hood sees in the world around her, it is not surprising that she should turn to traditional sources of order as a counterweight to the destructive forces of change that threaten stability and continuity.

In particular, Hood probes the nature of social "bonding," as her heroine in *Familiar Heat*, Faye Parry Rios, calls it at one point: the intricate network of affiliation, the social institutions and shared beliefs that make possible a cohesive and purposeful human existence and that underlie all productive social relationships. In the course of her exploration of the very fabric of human relationships, Hood leads the reader to ask a number of fundamental questions: what is the effect on human beings of living in a society such as that of modern America in which the continuity of values and beliefs, and even of the most elementary distinctions of value, seem to be under constant attack? In light of the destructive effects of such forces as modern skepticism and relativism, what sources of social stability and coherence remain? How can we restore a meaningful consensus regarding the purposeful nature of human life? How can we restore faith in the social institutions that are necessary to providing form and direction to human endeavors?

In its effort to address these large issues, *Familiar Heat* is a novel that tends toward the schematic structure of allegory and fairy tale. Faye Parry Rios' story of crisis and recovery is not merely the story of one individual; it is representative of a crisis within contemporary American culture as a whole, and the soul-searching in which Faye engages is the path to recovery for our culture. The novel's schematic structure, symbolic imagery, and dream symbolism connect *Familiar Heat* with the genre of allegory in which the surface events of the narrative point to or embody moral qualities. In essence, the novel is an ambitious attempt to respond to the compromised ethical milieu in which we all live at the beginning of the twenty-first century, as Hood works to convey the sense of how it is to live in a world that is unstable, faithless, and deeply confused about its purpose and direction. Few contemporary authors have peered as closely as this into the causes and effects of cultural amnesia, a collective mental damage not unlike Faye's, but, in this case, one that involves the disappearance not merely of one individual's mental capacities but of all that Western civilization has learned through thousands of years of thought and experience. At the same time, the society that Hood describes is one in which human beings are destroyed by the very things they have worked so hard to acquire: the sense of movement, affluence and excitement, and personal freedom that are the goals of modern American culture.

Loneliness, separation, disillusionment, and finally death follow on the heels of personal freedom, and from the beginning of her career, in her story collections, *And Venus Is Blue* and *How Far She Went*, Hood has set out to understand why. In *Familiar Heat*, the story of Faye and Vic Rios exemplifies this failure, as do the parallel stories of Cassia and Agapito Montevidez, Zeb and Palma Leonard, and others in the novel. The structure of the novel itself is an exact reflection of the theme: with the loosening of traditional restraints and discriminations, the various lives are connected only by casual and accidental relations, the sort of non-binding affiliations that are the norm in modern society. Vows, obligations, responsibilities—the more consequential foundations for affiliation—are all at risk in Hood's novel. In this milieu, the significance of human relationships seems to be in danger of being reduced to the transient and inconsequential level of cell phone chatter or anonymous e-mail communications. The binding obligations of family, marriage, or long service in one's profession are less and less common and increasingly unfamiliar and misunderstood, and with this loss of serious affiliation, there is an enormous spiritual price to pay. The psychic life that Hood describes all too often verges on the fearful and thin, yet it is also striving toward some dream of completion and order because of its underlying acknowledgment of loss. Hood's novel is a place of third marriages, of unconsummated longings, of momentary affairs, and of sudden death. Within such an environment, simply finding the words to describe one's condition is a challenge; making one's way back to a civilized life of dignity and purpose is a far more difficult task.

The task is even more daunting because the rich strata of myth that informed human existence in the past are largely absent. In a novel that has so much to do with fishing and that takes place in a community of Catholics, one might have expected Hood to develop the mythic symbolism of fishing—Christ as the fisher of souls; Simon Peter and Andrew, fishers of men; the legend of the fisher king—yet this and every other mythic suggestion are mitigated by the indifference of casual believers or the hostility of outright non-believers. To the extent that myth touches the lives of Hood's characters at all, it is often dismissed with a sort of embarrassment. The rich life-giving legacy of religious myth is an inheritance that many of Hood's characters have decided to reject.

Hood's style intentionally echoes this loss of depth in her characters, despite the allegorical structure of the novel as a whole in which a structure of anagogical meaning is developed. There is a striking thinness to the language and imagery of Hood's writing, just as there is to that of contemporary life. The beliefs held in common that once enriched the everyday lives of all in our civilization have been silenced as if by polite agreement; in our public institutions and national media, we are forbidden to speak of joy, hope, and faith. Even the Catholic priests in the novel, Father Ockham and Father Grattan, tread lightly in the way that they practice their vocation since they work among parishioners who, even if they continue to observe the rites of the church, do so only in a perfunctory manner.

The central character in *Familiar Heat* is Faye Parry Rios, a nineteen-year-old woman who finds her marriage in trouble even before her abduction during a bank robbery and her subsequent brutalization and rape. Following her terrible ordeal, Faye finds it difficult to return to everyday existence, and she and her husband drift further and further apart. They become estranged and eventually separate. Still, Faye refuses to divorce her husband, and this insistence on preserving her marriage is perhaps the first important indication of her commitment to traditional forms of affiliation. When her former high school boyfriend, Cristo Montevidez, suggests that "in the modern world" divorce is an option, Faye rejects the idea, telling him that "It's what I am. Married. I gave my word" (88). As Vic turns away from her, refusing to comfort her or even to communicate with her after the trauma of her rape, Faye turns increasingly for friendship to Cristo, now a famous pitcher with the Chicago Cubs. After three intense meetings during which they are drawn closer together, Faye realizes that she must break off the relationship, but at their final meeting she agrees to accompany Cristo to the airport where he must catch a plane for a ballgame in Atlanta. On the way to the airport, they suffer an automobile accident in which Cristo is killed and Faye is critically injured. The remainder of the novel tracks Faye's slow recovery from a condition in which her memory and even her speech and basic thought processes have been seriously damaged.

The mental damage that results from Faye's accident would seem to represent the extreme point of her estrangement from reality, but, in fact, it offers her a new possibility at life. After Faye wakes from a coma, Hood writes that "her memory slate [was] wiped clean" (186). This point of almost total amnesia is not the end, however, but a second chance to learn how to live and to establish a successful marriage. For this reason, Hood can write that "her innocence was like hope, like mercy" (188). As Joy A. Farmer writes, Hood's fiction focuses on "the existence of a love that redeems all human wickedness" (98), but the origin of this love cannot be found merely in souls of individual characters such as Faye: only the existence of an ultimate ground of goodness can explain the persistent choice by Hood's protagonists, even in a world of indisputable horror, of altruism and self-sacrifice. In the absence of an overriding template of values, discrete acts of goodness would be inexplicable.

The idea that Faye intends to reestablish her life on a firmer ground is closely connected with her interest in what she refers to as "facts"; she wishes to reconstruct her identity on the basis of what is certain, and this in a world in which most others seem to lead dishonest lives, lacking the simplicity and truthfulness that she demands. Faye is especially interested in geography and hopes eventually to learn everything about how other people live. As she reads and studies, Faye collects more and more "evidence," hoping that her world will become crystal clear, but she soon learns that the more evidence she collects, the more contradictions and ambiguities arise. As she discovers, she will need to graduate to a more complex form of knowledge—the more difficult order of knowledge that has to do with the imperfect nature of human beings, the motives of the human heart, and the ceaseless negotiations that comprise social existence. As she learns more about her own prior life, especially her marriage to Vic Rios, she finds that knowledge of the heart is the most difficult sort to obtain, if also the most rewarding. As a searcher for mere facts, she had abstained from drawing conclusions and making discriminations; now she must put her world back together by doing just that.

When Faye learns that she has indeed been married to "the Captain," Vic Rios, she realizes that it will be necessary for her to relearn an entirely new and more daunting subject. Her brief course at the church, "Preparing for

Life as an Adult," does little to educate her about marriage, so Faye considers requesting a book from the library on "bonding." Unable to find a book on this subject in the card catalogue, she calls the library from across the street to ask a "simple" but somewhat awkward question, "the difference...between love and sex" (326), but she hangs up before she is transferred to the reference desk. Still, since her own parents are deceased and she has no other family, the most important relationship that Faye must rebuild is that with her former husband and his family, and her question concerning the nature of bonding is completely apropos.

Faye's "reference question" is closely connected with Hood's main concern in *Familiar Heat*: the basis for stable and productive human relationships within a society that is deeply confused concerning the purposes and intentions of such relationships. This confusion is especially obvious in society's conception of marriage. One of the crucial scenes pertaining to Faye's marriage takes place in South Beach Park on the Fourth of July. There are pyrotechnics enough at the picnic even before the annual firework display takes place at the water's edge. Señora Rios, who is intent on having a grandson to carry on her husband's line, has planned a seemingly innocent family gathering with the ulterior motive of reuniting her son and daughter-in-law. Unfortunately, after Vic arrives with his current girlfriend, Marnie Fortner, a bitter quarrel between Marnie and Señora Rios takes place; then a fistfight between Vic and his brother, Tom, follows. While the picnic might seem a disaster, it actually serves as a turning point that leads to Vic's abandoning his girlfriend and eventually returning to Faye. Vic and Faye are not reunited in the melodramatic way that Vic's mother had hoped for—that is, against the backdrop of fireworks during the Fourth of July picnic—but they are reunited nonetheless.

Because of her insistence on understanding what others are content to leave ambiguous—including the genuine nature of marriage—throughout the novel Faye's character operates as a gauge of the disorientation of society around her. Unlike some others, especially her colleagues at the beauty parlor, she is unable simply to continue living in a milieu of what Farmer refers to as "familiar" demons (92)—the banality of evil that makes its appearance in commonplace settings. From the beginning scene in which Faye is horrified at the callous treatment of beached whales, she appears as a person of unusual sensitivity to questions of justice and decency. In this early scene, Faye comes upon a crowd of people who are horribly mistreating a family of whales that have beached on the shore, but there is nothing she can do to protect the whales from the heartless sightseers who wish to be photographed with the dying creatures or to cut "souvenirs" from them. In this scene, Hood establishes Faye's concern for all of life but especially for defenseless creatures as an ultimate value. It is not enough to live in the world as a bystander or a collector of "facts": one must engage life by making ethical distinctions and acting upon them. In her case, Faye is unfailingly kind to animals of all kinds and even seems to have a special gift of communicating with them. In a novel in which two of the major male characters make their living from fishing and in which Hood describes the agony of fish gasping for breath after they have been landed, her protagonist finds it difficult even to bait her own hook: indeed, she fishes with an unbaited hook, hoping not to catch anything. In this and other scenes, Faye senses her own close affiliation with wild animals; she is also an undomesticated creature who has been the subject of a brutal attack by a ruthless predator. Even though, as a human being, she must rely to some extent on the harvesting of nature, whether this harvest involves animal food or not, Faye practices an ethic of living humbly and acting as a good steward of the world around her—not merely of the environment but of human needs as well.

Faye is not only sensitive to the vulnerability of people and animals, she is also unusually sensitive to the physical settings in which she finds herself. She possesses the rare gift of sensing the appropriateness or inappropriateness of physical place—a sensitivity to place that goes well beyond what might be called good taste. What Faye is actually attempting, perhaps on an instinctive more than a conscious level, is a discrimination between a humane and gracious way of life and one that is merely efficient or convenient. It is not surprising that each of the various houses in which she lives has special significance. This is especially the case with Faye's "little cottage," the one-room house where she lives alone after she leaves rehab. Redecorating the house on a minimal budget is something of a challenge, but it brings out Faye's creativity. Discarded crates serve as coffee tables, and other furniture is acquired at little or no cost by scrounging throwaways or buying at thrift shops. The surest sign of Faye's instinct for beauty is the subtle and pleasing shade of pink—not really pink, she insists—with which she paints the outside of the home. In locating the right place to live and decorating it to express her true feelings, Faye ignores the objections of others and follows her vital instincts of joy and "life."

Many images in Hood's novel are similarly symbolic, from the seashore to the marsh, from the parish church to all of Faye's homes, and, in this way, Hood suggests that the places in which we live are far more than accidental and temporary quarters. It is necessary in some quite essential way that one live in the "right" place, and the place in which one lives becomes almost sentient in its vitality and meaningfulness. One of the reasons why the Florida setting in particular is so effective in *Familiar Heat* is that Hood wishes to write about essential matters and universal issues. The reduction of nature to sea, sky, sand, and marsh creates a sense of human beings living at an empty point in space where they face ultimate questions of the value and purpose of life.

Of course, Faye is not the only character in *Familiar Heat* who, in the face of a world of increasing alienation and indifference, is striving to protect the life around her and to create joy for herself and others, nor is she the only character who suffers the ordeals of fear and uncertainty. Cassia Montevidez, the mother of Faye's former boyfriend, Cristo, is another woman who has spent most of her life in a condition of anxiety and dread. A "navy brat" as a child, she has had to endure the uncertainty of her family's transfer from one assignment to another throughout a childhood of repeated dislocation. Perhaps as a result, she feels the need to maintain a sense of control, not only over her household but over all of her emotional life as well. As a consequence of this, Cassia finds it difficult to accept the fact that she is loved, as indeed she is by her adoring husband, Agapito. Everything she does is rooted in the fear of losing her grip on life, even her mysterious impulse to flee unexpectedly. Despite her husband's total devotion, she is never quite sure of her marriage. She finds it difficult to believe in love because her entire life has been one of broken relationships, and when her son, Cristo, dies in a car accident, she feels that she has been abandoned by a God who is angry at her for her unworthiness.

Like so many other characters in the book, Zeb Leonard lives in a fearful and uncertain environment, but in his case, he responds to confusion and loss in a positive and creative way—much the same way that Faye eventually does. Zeb finds purpose in his dream of becoming a boat captain, a dream that is rooted in his admiration for his father, and this certainly gives direction to his life. Still, there are many obstacles before Zeb can reach this goal. For one thing, as a result of his parents' deaths and his need to escape the oppressiveness of his guardian's farm, Zeb has relinquished any support that he might expect from his biological family. He has given up a familiar if arduous way of life and nearly all connection with his past. With so little connection to actual family members or a past way of life, Zeb suffers a sort of "memory loss" similar in its way to that of Faye, and like her he must create a new life out of what he can recover from the past.

Clearly, Zeb has a strong will to become a boat captain, but when his brother-in-law, Ben, is killed in the sinking of their newly acquired shrimp boat, Zeb's wife, Palma, blames him for her brother's death and demands that he give up his dream. Palma, who is pregnant with twins, also fears for

Zeb's life, and this is another reason she insists on his giving up his dream. Zeb and Palma are temporarily separated because of their disagreement over the shrimp boat, but Zeb never gives up hope of their being reunited. As he tells his son, Elven, the separation is only temporary. When he christens the refurbished boat, he chooses the name *Palma Forever*, a name that touches Palma's heart and leads to their reunion just at the point when their twins are born.

Eventually, Faye will establish a close relation with both Cassia Montevidez and Agapito, and with Zeb Leonard and Palma. In fact, during the course of her recovery Faye transforms herself into a far more open and receptive person than she had been even before the attack and the accident, and she finds new friends almost everywhere. Along with her receptivity to the troubled emotions of others, Faye also probes her own deepest feelings, which, she finds, are often not too different from those of others. When she encounters Father Grattan on the beach and studies the watercolors he has been painting, she realizes that she and the priest have experienced many of the same emotions. In Father Grattan's paintings, there are no living creatures, only the emptiness of sky and water. Like the pictures called "desolations" that Faye drew in rehab, Father Grattan's artwork signals an intense depression and isolation. Near the end of the book, he volunteers to accompany Tom and Vic to Cuba, sailing through a hurricane to recover the remains of their father, Oscar Carrasco Rios, a poet and hero of the anti-Castro forces. On the trip, not only do the three men recover the father's body, they also rescue a group of Haitian refugees. In doing so, Father Grattan recovers his connection with other people and regains a sense of purpose.

This kind of rediscovery, however, comes about only after facing the true desolation of contemporary existence. Because they have lost a knowledge of the mythological shape of their world, Hood's characters have difficulty in dealing with the major events of life. Marriage and birth are not sanctified. There is no comfort for grief, especially in the case of sudden death as that of Cristo Montevidez, the young baseball star who dies in his early twenties. At the service for Cristo, the priest's words from the traditional mass strike his mother, Cassia, as perverse. How can the priest speak of a "blessing" on the survivors of death? How can he ask Cassia to acknowledge God's mercy in the knowledge that Cristo is with his heavenly Father? Cassia's response is to question the church's teachings: "To take comfort, for in taking comfort, they who mourn are blessed. Hadn't the chaplain just said so? Why should she seek a blessing?" (107).

It is not just Hood's characters, however, who can be characterized as faithless. Hood's narrator plays an important part in the articulation of this ironic world, undermining whatever stability might otherwise exist by withholding judgment on the events being narrated. For example, a comment at the end of the passage that describes Zeb's lying to the police about his name and age undercuts the distinction between truth and lying: "So if it wasn't the truth, it wasn't really a lie. As for his age, what are a few years added on at the beginning, when you need them most" (158). This sort of moral equivocation is typical of Hood's narrator. One might compare the way that the narrator presents Cassia's repeated marital infidelities, which the narrator suggests might be excused because of Agapito's age and possible impotence. Never is the correct word, "adultery," used to describe her behavior. This accommodation suggests a narrator that is pandering to a modern audience and who shares the belief that evil does not exist and that moral distinctions cannot be made: to such a sensibility, all distinctions between true and false, good and bad, are factitious.

In an otherwise insightful survey of Hood's fiction, David Aiken mistakenly assumes that Hood's narrator—the "scrupulously unbiased reporter" of events in her fiction—can be equated with the author herself, a writer who, as Aiken conceives her, "leaves the reader no rights, no wrongs, or rules to follow" (26). As Aiken concludes, "Focused as they are on our common humanity, her stories bypass the issue of blame and carry the reader to a point where forgiveness is not only desirable but possible" (31). The problem with this analysis is that forgiveness cannot be accomplished in the absence of blame. The very notion of forgiveness requires an admission of guilt and acknowledgment that evil exists in the world. The sort of no-fault universe that Aiken imagines is incomprehensible if we wish to retain a concept of forgiveness. After all, one who commits outrages such as murder or rape but who is forgiven without acknowledging any wrongdoing would be free to commit the same crime an endless number of times—buoyed by the assurance that he will never be held accountable. Forgiveness must be preceded by genuine remorse and a sincere assurance to shun evil in the future. The process of confession, atonement, and forgiveness and its role in preventing future transgressions is eloquently explained by Leszek Kolakowski, who notes that the failure to acknowledge the objective existence of evil and, thus, the fact of human guilt leads to a state in which crimes are not only repeated but are, in fact, no longer distinguishable as crimes. In the absence of a clear distinction between good and evil and an insistence on the fact of guilt, there can be no restraint on those forces that would reduce society to anarchic conflict: "the ideal of total liberation is the sanctioning of force and violence and thereby, of despotism and the destruction of culture" ("Revenge" 73). The dismissal of evil as an objective fact carries dire consequences, and in any society it is always the weak who suffer the most from the consequences of moral indifference.

The question, then, is whether Hood, as author, also participates in the moral compromise of her narrator. Emphatically, she does not. The author is responsible for the creation of the novel as a whole, and in the book as a whole we see the horrific consequences of moral failure. Although characters are slow to perceive the connections, and though the narrator stands aside while evil is enacted, Hood makes evident the horrible damage that transpires as a result of society's inability to distinguish between good and evil.

One of the ways by which Hood signals her moral intentions in *Familiar Heat* is through the novel's performance of the woman's romance genre. As in the popular genre, Hood presents us with tales of women who define their existence in relation to men and, more specifically, in relation to the value in which they are held by men. Indeed, in an uncanny way, the plot structure of *Familiar Heat* parallels that of one of the most popular films of the 1990s, the same period in which it was composed. Like Lucy Moderatz, the protagonist of *While You Were Sleeping*, Faye Rios finds herself emotionally involved with two brothers. In the film, one of the brothers has apparently, though not actually, suffered memory loss similar to what Faye suffers. As in the film, while Faye is dealing with her attachment to one brother, she falls in love with the other, though she then returns to her original love, Vic. In the novel, one of the brothers—her true love—presents her with a globe that resembles the gift that Lucy received from her father. Like Faye, Lucy is a woman who is fascinated by geography but who has never traveled to any of the places she has dreamed of. As in the film, the story focuses at the end on the Cinderella-like marriage of the female protagonist and her prince.

Still, despite the many similarities between *Familiar Heat* and the woman's romance, Hood's novel is clearly not engaged in the sort of fantasy that characterizes the popular genre. If anything, Hood replicates the outlines of the romance genre in order to reflect on its shortcomings. After her recovery, Faye does not set out to garner the affection of a soul mate (though at one point she wonders if this is not exactly what she is doing, in relation, as it turns out, to the wrong man). She never defines her worth in relation to the admiration of men; she aspires to live within a universe made whole by friendships, activities, work, and study. This is not to say that Hood rejects the fundamental thesis of woman's romance, the belief that intimacy and commitment between men and women is one of the most important sources of fulfillment in life. In the end, *Familiar Heat* remains a romance, but its quest is for the grail of goodness and joy, not specifically for that of romantic love. As Faye implies in her inquiry concerning the nature of bonding,

Hood's romance concerns a form of affiliation that involves more than sexual or romantic love.

Genre romance, after all, is a form of escapism, and one of the overriding themes of *Familiar Heat* is the opposition between escapism and responsibility. The escape from history and from all that history suggests—the force of economics, politics, power, social institutions, and socialization itself—is the spurious goal of many characters in the novel. This escapist mentality has been dignified with a philosophical label, "libertarianism," (a word that dates to the beginning of the French Revolution) that intends to legitimize the withdrawal of the individual from society into an atomistic culture of personal choices. As in the watercolor paintings that Father Grattan produces after moving to Florida, art that expresses the priest's lack of connection with humanity, the ultimate result of a philosophy of radical individualism, is "aridity": the philosophy of libertarianism results in a pointless quest for self-enlargement and status at the expense of others and ultimately to the damage of the self. If we accept the idea that the ultimate goal of life is the complete autonomy of the individual, then existence becomes a thinly veiled form of competition among individual interests, and there is no basis other than temporary expediency for any form of affiliation; there is certainly no place for the sort of long-term need and obligation that is the basis of love.

Initially, we see that Faye, following the ordeals of abduction and rape and then of a horrific accident, wishes to rebuild her life on just such a principle of self-autonomy. For a time, she seems to prefer complete independence as she lives alone and unafraid in the cottage on the dead-end road, but all of this comes crashing down with her devastating dream of having to face the cold wind. In the dream she and a figure who appears to be Vic are "embracing," a tender moment of intimacy that is soon interrupted by distrust and separation. When she sees a ring on the man's hand—she is actually unsure whether it is Vic or Tom—she frees herself from him and runs away. She moves within a large crowd but turns in the other direction until she finds herself outside St. Francis Xavier parish church. She is then swept back toward the church by a frigid wind, and she is terrified by the fact that she is alone, separated from the crowd inside. After she wakes in terror from the dream, Faye turns on the lights in her house and notices Father Grattan's painting. She ponders the desolation that he has drawn and that she has retraced in her dream.

This dream has a profound effect on Faye's ability to deal with her fear of intimacy, especially the fear that follows her discovery that she is still legally married to Vic. After this dream, Faye realizes that, even with all that has happened to her, it is possible to recover a productive and meaningful life. Granted, the world is more complex than the set of "facts" that she initially relies on. Unlike facts, with their illusion of a pure and stable order, human beings are both corruptible and changeable. This is the lesson that experience has taught her in ample measure, but the alternative to living among others—the dream crowd that may include her mother—is a cold and self-destructive existence, a condition of total isolation and aridity. Faye immediately comprehends the meaning of her dream, and afterward we see a dramatic change in her life: she will draw closer to Vic and open her feelings to others as well; she will reenter the community, and she will rediscover a form of religious faith. She will also give birth to the grandchild that Vic's mother has wanted for so long, but only after Señora Rios passes away. Her dream thus marks Faye's new understanding of her relationship to the world; she is no longer fearful of others but no longer entirely self-reliant either. As she admits later, "It was an odd thing, to realize that her life was not just about her" (381).

Faye's husband, Vic, also has a dream that in its way seems to parallel her own, though it is far less detailed. He imagines being driven back to land unexpectedly during a storm. Not finding his wife waiting for him on the dock, he returns alone to the house that he shares with Faye. There he bumps up against her body hanging from the ceiling. He cuts her down but wakens before he sees her face. Since Vic has been evading responsibility for his wife for some time, perhaps fleeing from his own deep emotions regarding the ordeals that she has suffered, it would seem that his dream implies his sense of guilt over the abandonment of his wife. He realizes that Faye has been struggling to regain her identity, even her knowledge of simple everyday matters, but he has repeatedly turned away from her. At the same time, he may feel anger concerning the disruption of their normal lives that the attack and accident have caused.[1]

Both dreams may be symbolic of the sterility of an isolated existence or of the emptiness of the future in the absence of close attachments. The dream crisis rescues Faye from the quest for self-autonomy as she now admits an instinctive need for friendship and even love, and she displays a need to reconnect with the past. In this sense, Faye is reaching toward those very sorts of traditional values that are most at risk in her society: the sanctity of marriage, respect for parents, devotion to country and community, all of which are grounded on belief in a purposeful life and ultimately dependent on belief in a transcendent order of being. As she plays the audiotapes that her mother made before her death, Faye reflects on her ancestral history—the fact that her mother was half-Vietnamese and grew up speaking Vietnamese and French—and Faye decides to study French in order to reconnect with this history. From one of her mother's friends, Faye acquires the rocking chair that her mother used during Faye's infancy. This chair still holds the marks of her mother's body where it wore down the surface, and it now fits Faye's body just as it did her mother's. The chair is a powerful symbol of the need to summon her mother back to life and to connect her own life with that of her mother. This instinct toward the recovery of knowledge of the past leads Faye back not only to the study of French and to the use of inherited furniture but toward moral attitudes and modes of rationality passed down from parent to child.

In reality, though, there are contradictory forces at work in Faye's character, just as there are in contemporary American culture: the impulse toward radical freedom—the desire simply to be left alone that rules much of suburban mores—in conflict with responsibilities to family, friends, colleagues, and total strangers. Like Robinson Crusoe, Faye has been shipwrecked on a desolate island of pure individualism, but unlike Crusoe, Faye shows little inclination to remain on that island once the consequences of her isolation become apparent. Despite her culture's credo of individual autonomy, Faye, like most of Hood's major characters, is drawn to the exact opposite of the libertarian position: Faye gradually rediscovers the depth of feeling that drew her to Vic Rios in the first place, and she reenters a busy life of associations that are grounded in concern for other people and for her world as a whole.

The conclusion of the novel reunites all of the estranged lovers after the manner of a Shakespearean tragicomedy. (One thinks of *The Tempest* or *The Winter's Tale*.) Cassia and Agapito are drawn closer together as over time the sharp edge of Cassia's grief passes and as her husband, who suffers increasingly from senility, requires more of her care. At the end, Cassia and Agapito find that they are dependent upon one another, not just for the care that Agapito requires, but, more importantly, for the deep love that they express for one another. Touchingly, Agapito does not allow Cassia to leave his side, and they exchange repeated vows of love and fidelity as Agapito asks in Spanish, *Querida?*, and Cassia answers, "Here." Zeb and Palma are also reunited, and it is evident that they have reestablished a close family, now with three children. Most importantly, of course, Faye and Vic find their love not only restored but greatly strengthened. The home that they build—Faye's third since her marriage—is a reflection of their new-found respect and willingness to compromise. After Vic adamantly refuses to return to their former house, the one "with the blue roof," they build a house with "the Caribbean style and Key West shutters" (451)—a style that suits them both. In this setting, one that carries none of the baggage of their months of separation, they embark on a lifetime of marriage, parenthood, friendship, and work that sets them apart from the cultural anarchy that surrounds them. Their new home, with the "old-fashioned look," is an ideal setting for a marriage that stands apart in a world of uncertainty and fear.

Note

1 Tom also has a significant dream regarding Faye. He comes across Faye in the woods and then sees a fire approaching from the ocean. As the flames sweep over Faye and himself, Tom covers her body and saves her from the fire, but when they return to the shelter, Faye walks separately, gliding easily over the thick undergrowth like a butterfly while Tom struggles to make his way. At the shelter, Tom finds Faye with a group of people in a beautiful, almost perfect little room. Tom is handed a damaged painting, but he is unable to repair it and returns it to the clerk. Tom feels that he must leave the hall and complete an important errand, one that seems to be connected with the sea, but when an alarm is set off, Tom only stands facing the sea in confusion. His dream retraces his entire relationship with Faye: his protection of her after she leaves rehab, their growing intimacy, her flight from him and toward new friends and toward Vic, and his coming "errand" of recovering his father's remains from Cuba.

8

Naipaul's Grief:
The Enigma of Arrival

Reflecting on his birthplace in Trinidad, a small town named Chaguanas, V. S. Naipaul pointed to its long and sometimes violent history of colonization, noting that "the world is always in movement. People have everywhere at some time been dispossessed" ("Nobel Prize Lecture"). In the case of his hometown, its indigenous people had been completely wiped out by the Spanish, who were then defeated by the British, who were, in turn, disempowered by the independence movement following World War II. So it is with all places, even those that seem most confident in their power and prestige. Whether it comes suddenly by way of conquest or gradually through the insidious process of displacement or cultural decay, eventually change comes to every civilization. Every place on earth where humans live in any numbers has been occupied before by a different people; all people will at some point be displaced or subjugated, and each turn of fortune is apt to be accompanied by human suffering on a large scale. It is a dismal scenario, one that we cannot escape, but one that perhaps we can retard. How to slow the process of disorder, how to postpone the inevitable crisis—this is the question that haunts Naipaul's fiction, and it perhaps receives its most profound treatment in his 1987 novel, *The Enigma of Arrival*. The hard-won product of a painful self-examination, this novel reflects Naipaul's long habit of self-restraint, his searing commitment to truth, and his care for every detail of art, especially for the seemingly insignificant, distasteful, or upsetting aspects of everyday life. Out of this arduous labor, Naipaul comes to understand the world of escapism, self-delusion, and sham in which his contemporaries seem to revel. Knowing that no matter how great his talent or his efforts he cannot reform an entire civilization bent on destruction, Naipaul is left with a profound sense of grief for what has been lost and, more frightening, an inescapable terror of what lies ahead.

The Enigma of Arrival is fiction in the guise of autobiography, autobiography in the service of a new narrative form that reaches beyond fiction of a conventional sort. An account of how Naipaul as a young man arrived in England, bringing with him an antiquated education in British literary classics and little else in the way of real knowledge of human beings, the novel details his struggle to support himself while he finds his way as a writer. Living in a small cottage on a neglected estate in the west of England, the tenant of a reclusive but seemingly benevolent landlord, Naipaul has arrived at the temporary home where he will reside during his most productive years. From this new base of operations—like so much else in his life, a temporary refuge from life's fearful impermanence—Naipaul immediately begins a sort of cultural archeology into the many layers of British history that are evident in the physical and cultural ruins that surround him. Following a logic that reaches back in time to forces and motives that the author only vaguely understands, the near present of the novel's opening pages reverts to earlier periods of his life: his childhood as a competitive pupil in Trinidad, his education at Oxford on a prized scholarship, his lonely years of struggle as he pursues his ambition to become a professional writer, and his long fear of poverty and ruin even after the publication of his first books. Yet this retrospective narrative, necessary as it is in a way, is gradually supplanted by an overlapping account that details a more essential identity, what we may simply call the author's "character." This is an identity that transcends the accidents of historical background and that seeks to understand in a more fundamental way the relationship of self to world.

The importance of "character" in this sense cannot be overestimated. Naipaul's entire professional life has been a struggle to retain his individuality within an intellectual culture in which one's social or ethnic origins limit and even determine identity. From the beginning, Naipaul recognized the dishonesty of this conception of social identity even as it gained more and more influence during his lifetime. As Naipaul wrote during his visit to Peronist Argentina during the 1970s, "Where jargon turns living issues into abstractions, and where jargon ends by competing with jargon, people don't have causes. They only have enemies" (qtd. in "Nobel Prize Lecture"). Identity politics does not further the interests of the group that it intends to promote, just the opposite. By advancing a particular group on the assumption of past injustices, it denies that group a genuine role in the historical present. In his own case, Naipaul has found his work both dismissed and embraced for the wrong reasons: initially regarded as a mere regional or local color writer, an author of inconsequential miniatures of a picturesque but unsophisticated place, he was later sought out as an authority on colonial repression.

Rather than accept this reduction to an ideologically determined identity,

Naipaul submitted himself to an arduous literary apprenticeship that demanded a complete devotion to the truth of actual experience. A good part of his development as an artist and as a person involved the recognition that his formal schooling had been a "half-education" (*Enigma* 245) and that he must educate himself through the humbling exaction of his art. In this discipline, the author is refashioned; the personal self, with all its baggage of social and racial self-consciousness, is subjugated to a humanizing tradition of reason and observation. In particular, the enormous racial sensitivity that Naipaul has brought with him to Britain must be suppressed: racial vulnerability is "not the kind of personality the writer wishes to assume" (*Enigma* 124).

In *Enigma*, Naipaul's dedication is contrasted with the self-indulgence of his friend, Allen, an unsuccessful writer living in London. Although Allen, the author of radio book reviews and other short programs, conveys the impression that he is privately engaged in some "big project," a "large book" that will redeem his life, he is actually producing almost nothing. In the literary culture that Allen so readily embraces, no large books or even good books can be written because there is no restraint regarding the ideological positions that control intellectual discourse and, thus, suppress originality of any sort. Within a culture in which all insights are self-censored before they are fully formed, no authentic art can survive. Still, the point of this anecdote is not to advance our opinion of Naipaul by drawing invidious comparisons with a former associate: it is to show how dangerous it is to substitute ideological correctness for the hard labor of artistic creation or any other sort of cultural work. The revelation of Allen's suicide, the final event in an inconsequential and pointless life, is meant to suggest the self-destructive inertia that dominates modern literary and academic culture.

For Naipaul, writing constitutes something else entirely: more than anything, it is a discipline in exactness and perception. In his pursuit of truth, Naipaul challenges conventional assumptions concerning aesthetic taste as well as assumptions concerning social identity. By virtue of its very existence, *Enigma* tests our conception of what a fictional narrative should be: it is hardly a conventional work of realism, nor is it a book that can be understood in the now-familiar terms of modernist or postmodernist aesthetics. Unlike the sort of naturalism that reduces art to merely registering the least beautiful and noble of human actions—an aesthetic that in our time plays out in the films of Martin Scorsese or, at a greater extreme, of Paul Verhoeven—Naipaul's writing assumes the tempering presence of a discriminating mind. The author does not merely record; he records and judges. Narrative is not only a perception of a social reality that is, by virtue of its indiscriminate presentation, implicitly deterministic—the unfamiliar, disturbing sights that a studious immigrant from Trinidad might record over a period of forty years abroad—it is qualified on every page by the author's convictions. The qualities that Naipaul admires in Thomas Mann's *The Magic Mountain* are those that we find in his own work: there is "concern" and "wonder," and "annihilating violation" ("The Documentary Heresy" 23).

Naipaul is the most wary of writers because, more so than any of his contemporaries, he understands the cultural limitations and pressures of his age. As a result, Naipaul's fiction is both refreshingly unconventional and large in its ambitions. Its impulse is not to critique what exists—the reflexive urge to unmask and expose the conspiratorial heart of Western civilization that has become a cliché of our culture—but to understand the limitations within which human beings live and to affirm their efforts to create decency and worth. Naipaul's intentions certainly do not involve the "essential traits" of "doubt, disbelief, scepticism, instinctive mistrust" (47) that Jeffrey Meyers detects in his work; it is the modernists who exhibit these reductive qualities. Even a writer of the stature of Joyce was, in Naipaul's opinion, "not universal…a man of so little, so little imagination, able to record the life around him in such a petty way" ("Words"). In his compulsive focus on degradation and ugliness, a destructive focus that reflects the philosophical cynicism of his times, Joyce mirrors the pettiness of modernist culture. Above all, Joyce evinces an arrogant detachment from ordinary human beings, an alienation from general existence that replicates one of the dominant features of modernist practice.

By contrast, Naipaul's habit of discrimination is tied to a fierce honesty that works to place his own existence within the world as it is. Following the demands of his art, he evaluates and re-evaluates his own assumptions, a habit engendered in his need to comprehend the ritualized lives of the Indian community in Trinidad. This community, as Naipaul recounted in his Nobel lecture, was "incapable of self-assessment, which is where learning begins." To comprehend his role within the cosmopolitan culture to which he immigrated was even more difficult, for it involved acquiring knowledge and making judgments about a complex civilization that was not only unfamiliar to him but that was also deeply uncertain of its own purposes. Assessing his own motives and admitting that he lived in a world of disorder and flux was a crucial part of his task. However tentative and approximate, the author's ability to see the world whole and to arrive at judgments is all that stands between a life of dignity and purpose and its opposite: the decline into decay, madness, *acedia,* the surrender to indifference and cynicism that seem the direction toward which post-imperial England and America are headed.

In the allegory of cultural decline that constitutes *The Enigma of Arrival*, it is fitting that the estate on which Naipaul has lived so contentedly and productively should at the end be overrun by vandals and marauders who are the direct descendants of those who once labored with dedication and skill on the same estate. The descendants of those who once lived with faith in a purposeful universe and who were thus willing to sacrifice so much of themselves in the interests of their vocations now seem to be motivated by pure self-interest or, what is worse, by a contemptuous distaste for all that is beautiful or noble: they are carried along by the malicious instinct "to reduce [their surroundings] to junk" (*Enigma* 325). What is missing, quite simply, is the authority of belief that exacts effort and dedication. The lack of faith in any outward authority, not just the external authority of government or law but the authority of an idea that might elicit their devotion to excellence, turns skilled craftsmen into vandals.

At the time of his first arrival in Britain in 1950, Naipaul faced not only the difficult adjustment to an unfamiliar culture but, what was more daunting, the adjustment of his preconceptions of Britain, the land of beauty and grace that he had imagined from his reading, to the reality of a demoralized nation in the throes of cultural change. This "strange and unknown" land becomes all too real after his arrival at a shabby Earl's Court boardinghouse in London, a place filled with "the flotsam of Europe" (*Enigma* 141), none of them the "metropolitan" types that he had hoped to expropriate for his fictional material. In fact, the other residents at Earl's Court, especially the Italian waitress, Angela, who becomes his first friend in Britain, are nearly all newcomers struggling to make ends meet. Yet, so intent is Naipaul on uncovering the Britain of his dreams that he fails to notice the actual Britain before his eyes. He learns nothing of Angela really until thirty years later when a letter arrives from her, a letter that Naipaul never answers. What the letter summons up is a memory of Angela's "instability," an "unsettling" memory that Naipaul wishes to repress (*Enigma* 178).

By coincidence, Angela's letter arrives at a point when Naipaul is composing fiction that deals with a similar "restless and uncertain" (*Enigma* 179) generation of young people searching for truth in a simplistic new religion. Naipaul understands that characters like Pitton attempt to fill a similar vacuum of faith by turning to fraudulent forms of cult religion: the sort of ad hoc belief systems that are increasingly evident in modern culture as traditional belief systems are discarded. This sort of conversion, involving the rejection of all that one has inherited and the uncritical submission to an unfamiliar ritual, is "a great neurosis, the rejection of all that one is, all that one stands for" ("Words"), yet it is all too commonplace in contemporary culture. The rise of cult sensibility is clearly the result of a felt need to substitute newly invented faiths for traditional systems of belief that no longer garner conviction, and the more rapid the pace of social change, the less able traditions are to maintain credibility. Ranging from religious cults organized around a particular leader to extremist movements and utopian experiments, these systems also include psychic and mystical orders, New Age faiths, and even the cult-like following of sports teams. With the hybrid social realm supplanting the private and public realms, ad hoc systems of belief tend to be located within the murky field of the social. What was once positioned within the imposing public institution of the church is now often regarded in apologetic tones as something akin to a hobby, a practice involving neither devout private faith nor shared public ritual. Moreover, it should be pointed out that such cult-like systems compel belief only to the extent that they are willed by the self. Lacking the force of tradition with its sense of legitimacy backed by generations of allegiance, modern ad hoc systems enjoy only the support of social consensus, a popular will that is subject to constant revision. Those who give credence to Jungian analysis today may, and probably will, find conviction in another fashionable system tomorrow; those who adhere to a skeptical secularism now may easily be recruited into a dangerous personality cult in the future. With no authority beyond the self and the self's prerogative to decide, one may choose any ground of belief and one may change grounds as often as one wishes.

The need for an authority outside of their own appetites and impulses is painfully apparent among all of the characters in Naipaul's fiction and particularly so in *Enigma*, but authority, if it is to be anything but a travesty of conviction, must emerge from one's own historical traditions. Naipaul's own salvation stems from the realization that he possesses the "cultural memory," so to speak, necessary to withstand the dramatic decline taking place around him. He is able to perceive what he does and to discriminate good from evil because of his training in and respect for a particular tradition of values. This tradition stresses education, industriousness, social stability, moderation, loyalty, and self-restraint, among other things. Naipaul also recognizes the crucial importance of legal protection of individual rights, especially the right of free speech and that of private property, for without such protections the individual is subject to forms of intimidation that open the way for tyranny, whether that of authoritarian rule or mob anarchy.

Naipaul's values, then, are essentially those of Western liberal democracy, a civilization that affords a unique balance of tolerance and order, and yet Naipaul recognizes that all civilizations exist in a state of continual development and change. As the product of thousands of years of classical and Judeo-Christian culture, the democratic culture that he most values, the product of many layers of influence, faces a unique challenge today. Despite its achievement of offering the greatest degree of freedom, prosperity, and security of any previous civilization, liberal democracy is under attack not only by those who oppose Western civilization from outside but, paradoxically, by those who are its most direct beneficiaries: those who have grown up in the affluence and freedom of the West. In place of the precious inheritance that they have received, they seem intent on substituting a world ruled by anarchy, ignorance, and destruction. *Enigma* is Naipaul's exploration of this paradox, the betrayal of the West by its own sons and daughters, the selling of the birthright for an illusory sense of emancipation and free will.

No single individual, of course, can rescue a civilization intent on self-destruction; he can only remind his readers of the value of the cultural traditions that they are in the process of discarding and cause them to reflect on the destructiveness of their heedless rejection of the past. In *Enigma*, many of the tropes and actions of the novel are intended to convey Naipaul's sense of wanton destruction, and one of the symbols used to depict the contemporary decay of conviction is the ivy that covers many of the buildings and trees on the Wiltshire estate where he lives. Covering the old flint building across from Naipaul's rented cottage and clinging to many of the trees around the manor of his once-wealthy landlord, ivy presents a lovely front but, like all untruth, its effect is to hasten the destruction of whatever it is intended to adorn. Ivy, then, suggests delusion as well as dissolution, and romance—one of the cult-like surrogates for authentic belief that has come to dominate our culture. By its very nature romance is ivy-like: it is a lovely and pleasing façade that will, in time, be found insubstantial.

In a similar way, the events of the novel suggest the damaging effects of the cult of romance. The important anecdote that recounts Brenda's affair with Michael Allen, the ambitious, handsome young contractor, reveals the degree to which human beings, once they have discarded the restraints of a traditional belief system, can find themselves reduced to brutishness. In running off to meet Michael in Italy—a romantic adventure that seems to have been scripted by her culture's worship of personal self-gratification as an ultimate value—Brenda behaves without concern for her husband, Les, a lawn worker employed on the estate. Her shallow imagination, perhaps inspired by film romances, nonetheless invokes fatal consequences: after the return from Italy following her rejection by Allen, Brenda is murdered by her distraught spouse.

The wholesale discarding of one's cultural tradition not only leaves one without a basis for self-awareness, it also eliminates the possibility of a common belief system that might regulate one's relationship to others. In a novel that serves to such an extent as a cautionary tale, far more is shown of the failure of these relationships than of their success. Still, in the Naipaul persona himself, and in his relations with his friends—the "protective" Phillipses, and especially Jack, the last of the professional gardeners—we see something of the positive potential of Naipaul's vision. The first important relationship that Naipaul's narrator establishes in Wiltshire is with Jack, a person who becomes, in Naipaul's mind, the representative of an earlier, more stable period before World War I. Jack, who "lived among ruins, among superceded things" (*Enigma* 15), is a skilled gardener with an intimate knowledge of traditional lore and one who turns his back on all modern "advances" in communication and transportation. As Naipaul writes, "I saw his life as genuine, rooted, fitting: man fitting the landscape. I saw him as a remnant of the past" (*Enigma* 15).

The perception of Jack as an "authentic" rural figure within an idyllic traditional landscape is created by the perceiver, specifically by the literary preconceptions of agrarian Britain that Naipaul absorbed from childhood reading, especially from Wordsworth and Romantic poetry. Unfortunately, this perception must soon be revised as Naipaul tells us that Jack has actually been "living in the middle of junk, among ruins" (*Enigma* 15) during his entire life. In fact, Jack's life has been much more complex than the narrator at first supposes, migratory in its own way just as Naipaul's has been and undermined by the rapid change taking place throughout the twentieth century. Jack's careful devotion to his work and his sense of reserve and dignity in his personal life are his bulwark against the dizzying pace of social change, and they also identity him as a civilized man, one who chooses to live by the positive values that he has inherited from the past. The traditional quality that Naipaul at first discerns in Jack actually exists, but it turns out to be something more essential than the legacy of Old England as Naipaul has understood it from the British classics: it is the virtue of a free but cautious human being, a person worthy of respect because of his ability to live an independent existence and to see life whole.

Jack is the figure in *The Enigma of Arrival* who most resembles Naipaul himself, and both discover the redeeming force of the mythical, if not actual, reality of a small-scale, agrarian ideal of society. Like Flannery O'Connor, though not invoking a specifically religious myth, Naipaul recognizes that ideals of justice and virtue are as central to his task as a writer, as they are to his life as a person. Without an ethical perspective on the world, his fiction would have no shape or meaning. There would be no basis for a distinctive vision of existence, and there would be no resolution to any conflict since, in the absence of a systematic moral understanding, all solutions would be equally relevant.

It is from a particular moral perspective that Naipaul is able to discern the steady decline taking place on the Wiltshire estate, and this portrayal is intended to reflect what is taking place in Britain as a whole. As some of the estate's land is sold off and fenced in, what little connection exists among those who live and work in the area is lost. It is a social connection that Naipaul, in spite of his very private nature, has sought on his daily walks. The act of enclosing those areas that for centuries have served as public passages has the effect of further reducing the individual's connection with others; this restriction of movement severs the individual from the community and, more significantly, undermines the continuity of shared attitudes and values, thus breaking down the traditional sense of life that had governed for centuries. It was by way of routine interactions, meetings as seemingly inconsequential as those that occurred daily on the common areas, that distinctions concerning the nature of one's relationship to the community—as well as to much else, to one's work, family, politics, law, and mores—were defined, confirmed, and reinforced. Much of this local discourse has now been superceded by what takes place in the forum of a standardized national media, and such discourse is not only homogeneous but necessarily alien to local attitudes and innately undemocratic by virtue of the media's total control of the discourse, which cannot be challenged by the passive viewer. Once individuals come to see themselves as existing outside the local norms and expectations that have guided them in the past, there is no restraint to their actions, for their actions are then based either on private conceptions of value or on ill-fitting solutions disseminated by the national media.

The fencing off of the commons contributes to a growing sense of isolation, but equally important is the inhuman scale that has spread through all aspects of life, from commerce and industry to housing and city planning. The increasing anonymity of life on the estate, the replacement of skilled gardeners by those who manage the farming for efficiency alone and who may no longer even live on the estate, is one indication of a drift toward impersonal organization. The lesson of Jack's greenhouse, or for that matter the new dairy, both of which were built "on too big a scale, a scale too big for men" (*Enigma* 84), is that architecture, like all else that touches human existence, must conform to a proper, innately human scale. The inhuman scale that Naipaul finds objectionable is party to "a new way of farming, logic taken to extremes, the earth stripped finally of its sanctity" (*Enigma* 59). Logic in place of nature; efficiency violating sanctity; selfishness and greed driving out beauty: this is Naipaul's vision of the new order of things.

Naipaul has always recognized the impermanent nature of human civilizations, and the new order—life organized on a scale and at a pace unknown in the past—may be inescapable, but the "pillage" that he now witnesses on the Wiltshire estate engenders a keen sense of grief. It is not merely the fact that he is forced to quit the refuge that he has come to cherish or that his illness has brought on a new awareness of his own mortality. Naipaul grieves for humanity, for he has seen how easily a civilization with values of decency and tolerance—that of modern Britain and other Western democracies—can decline into an inhuman culture based only on self-gratification and consumption. In spite of all his efforts, his enormous talent, and his luck, Naipaul is now overcome by grief, and, as he relates near the end of the novel, it is "with a new awareness of death that I began at last to write. Death was the motif; it had perhaps been the motif all along" (*Enigma* 344).

Only toward the end of the novel does Naipaul recount how he finally began to compose the story of his time spent on the manor, an account that is of crucial importance because it explores the artist's purpose and motivation. The impetus to write comes after he attends the funeral of his sister, who has died prematurely and whose death makes him intensely aware of "the grief and the glory" of human life (*Enigma* 354). Impelled by this loss, Naipaul begins to write about Jack, the estate gardener with whom he seems to identify in many ways. Now Naipaul discovers that far more is involved in a single, ordinary life—his own or that of another—than he might have supposed. In this novel, whose structure is an endless cycle of destruction and rebirth, Naipaul returns from this end point of the narrative to the beginning and from the fact of death to the "glory" of Jack's life. Perhaps only at the end do we realize how consequential this life has been, especially in its example of steadfast resistance to the growing abstraction of modern consciousness. This resistance mirrors Naipaul's own, and like Jack, Naipaul preserves his integrity at the cost of exclusion and misinterpretation. Like that of his creator, Jack's life exhibits a selfless courage, even a sort of religious quality: not, of course, the religion of church or dogma, but nonetheless a faith in the immaterial presence of goodness without which civilization is doomed. In this way, Jack's life has not been the uneventful "idyll" that Naipaul assumes it to have been; it has been a heroic struggle to preserve truth and beauty in a time of confusion and disorder. As Naipaul comes to understand, Jack's life is far more eventful than even he could have imagined.

The contemplation of a single life in the manner in which Naipaul conducts it leads to much greater insight than if it had been the production of an author whose work is controlled by a narrow ideology. In Naipaul's view, politics, if it is to be more than a mere exercise in jargon and rhetoric, would necessarily begin with the experience of a single human being. The political engagement that Naipaul's critics seem to require of fiction writing would relegate the individual to the mass and thus diminish the significance of that individual's experience. A great deal of recent fiction and criticism makes just that assumption: through its reflexive reduction of individuals to race, class, and gender (or whatever other categories we wish to focus on), the private experience of an individual—friendship, reading, love of nature, reflection—is treated as having practically no value. Unfortunately, by this process the truly political act, that of a mind at liberty to reflect and choose freely, has been lost sight of. In Saul Bellow's phrase, the "forms and signs"—the "old words" of "honor" and "compassion" and "hope," "desire," "grief"— have been "suppressed" (238). Like Bellow, and like William Faulkner (whose Nobel address Bellow appears to be paraphrasing in the passage above), Naipaul is attempting to speak once again of desire and grief, honor and compassion and hope. Naipaul's great accomplishment is not only his fidelity to art but, more importantly, his fidelity to humane civilization, not merely Western civilization but the potential for any sort of civilization based on enduring traditions of thought and belief.

Naipaul's accomplishment, it should be stressed, does not constitute an attempt to return to older systems of order in precisely the forms that they took in the past. Akash Kapur's idea that Naipaul "has too stubbornly espoused a blinkered ethic of historical preservation" ("Neuroses") is profoundly mistaken, for Naipaul's writing is about nothing so much as the inevitability of change and the necessity of acceptance of life in the midst of change. Naipaul is fully aware of the fact that the past cannot be preserved intact: decay is as much a part of the universe as is birth and growth. This knowledge was apparent to Naipaul from his childhood experience in Trinidad, for the India from which his grandfather came, as he notes at the beginning of *An Area of Darkness*, could never have been reconstituted in the Caribbean or passed down to the children of immigrants, nor could it be preserved over time even in the Indian homeland. In his Nobel lecture, Naipaul mocks the notion that in Trinidad, the Indian people "had brought a kind of India with us, which we could, as it were, unroll like a carpet on the flat land." There was almost no transference of the particular practices of Indian culture from Naipaul's grandparents to him, and the attempts of some to maintain Indian customs and rituals at all cost were forced, unreal gestures. The lesson of Naipaul's childhood narratives, his journey to India, and his entire meditation on exile is the insistence that exile cannot be ameliorated: it is our condition, and any denial or resort to fantasies of "home" will prove destructive. There is no way back, and the only way forward is through the ruthless admission of our condition, facing it, as he says, with "humour and pity," yet humor and pity, like the old verities that Faulkner cites, are the legacy of a past civilization that survives in the sensibility of traditionalists such as Naipaul, Faulkner, and O'Connor. Regardless of whether we conceive of these verities as associated with a "return," they constitute a significant form of continuity with the past because they continue to embody a particular civilization's conception of a spiritual and moral order. One can never preserve the past unchanged, nor would one want to, but, on the other hand, the effect of utter discontinuity is mental incoherence and ultimately madness.

A coherent understanding of existence, in opposition to the forces of doubt and confusion that seem to dominate contemporary culture, is the objective of all of Naipaul's writing. Out of the decay—the mold and rot of time and life itself—his work professes a renewed sense of order born out of an awareness of the damage of radical forms of skepticism and relativism. His fiction is a bulwark against disorder and anarchy, against injustice and madness, and against the emptiness and spite toward which human beings tend in the absence of any purposeful order. Out of his grief, Naipaul enjoins us to live again as free individuals. In the midst of despair and decay, his fiction is meant to encourage a resistance similar to his own. In an interview with Tarun Tejpal, Naipaul insisted, "Good writing requires a moral view of the world" ("Words"). A reading of Naipaul's fiction exhorts the reader as well to restore a "moral view" to the world, and ultimately this is Naipaul's gift of hope to us.

Nonetheless, if there is hope, there is also grief in abundance. In *Enigma*, the transformation of the manor from a Victorian estate with its large and dedicated staff into a modern enterprise operated by a handful of self-serving, diffident salaried employees suggests in microcosm the larger transformation of Western culture: lives more and more solitary, without shared beliefs, lacking a network of family or true friends, living more and more fearful lives in isolated spaces in which electronic media are the only connection with the larger world. The genius of Naipaul's vision is to make us see that these lives are the tragic legacy of a debased philosophical system rooted in despair. Seemingly without import, these suburban lives mark a turning point in the cultural history of the West since they are the first tangible evidence of the failed philosophy of rebellion. In our reaction, we share Naipaul's grief, but his art also calls us to a sense of renewal: to salvage as much as possible from what has been lost, to return to a place where, as Flannery O'Connor urged, we can "recover our simplicity," taking seriously those questions of virtue, beauty, and justice that are at the center of Naipaul's vision.

Bibliography

Agee, James. *Agee on Film: Criticism and Comment on the Movies.* New York: Modern Library, 2000.
———. *A Death in the Family.* New York: Bantam, 1969.
———. "Dream Sequence." *Agee: Selected Literary Documents.* Troy, NY: Whitson, 1996. 264–72.
———. *Letters of James Agee to Father Flye.* 2nd ed. New York: Ballantine, 1971.
Agee, James, and Walker Evans. *Let Us Now Praise Famous Men.* Boston: Houghton Mifflin, 1941.
Aiken, David. "Mary Hood: The Dark Side of the Moon." *Southern Writers at Century's End.* Ed. Jeffrey J. Folks and James A. Perkins. Lexington: UP of Kentucky, 1997. 21–31.
Arendt, Hannah. *The Portable Hannah Arendt.* Ed. Peter Baehr. New York: Penguin, 2003.
Armour, Robert A. "History Written in Jagged Lightning: Realistic South vs. Romantic South in *The Birth of a Nation.*" *The South and Film.* Ed. Warren French. Jackson: UP of Mississippi, 1981. 14–21.
Bacon, Jon Lance. *Flannery O'Connor and the Cold War Culture.* Cambridge: Cambridge UP, 1994.
Barson, Alfred T. *A Way of Seeing: A Critical Study of James Agee.* Amherst: U of Massachusetts P, 1972.
Bellow, Saul. *Mr. Sammler's Planet.* Greenwich, CT: Fawcett, 1970.
Bergreen, Laurence. *James Agee: A Life.* New York: Penguin, 1984.
Brooks, Cleanth. *On the Prejudices, Predilections, and Firm Beliefs of William Faulkner.* Baton Rouge: Louisiana State UP, 1987.
Canetti, Elias. *Crowds and Power.* New York: Farrar Straus Giroux, 1962.
———. *The Human Province.* New York: Farrar Straus Giroux, 1978.
Cash, Jean W. *Flannery O'Connor: A Life.* Knoxville: U of Tennessee P, 2002.
Day, Douglas. "Borges, Faulkner, and *The Wild Palms.*" *Virginia Quarterly Review* 56 (Winter 1980): 107–18.
Desmond, John. "Flannery O'Connor's Misfit and the Mystery of Evil." *Renascence: Essays on Values in Literature* 56.2 (2004): 129–39.
Dickens, Charles. *Little Dorrit.* London: Thomas Nelson and Sons, n.d.
Dobbs, Cynthia. "Flooded: The Excesses of Geography, Gender, and Capitalism in Faulkner's *If I Forget Thee, Jerusalem.*" *American Literature* 73.4 (2001): 811–35.
Donaldson, Scott. "Scott Fitzgerald's Romance with the South." *Southern Literary Journal* 5.2 (1973): 3–17.
Edmunds, Susan. "Through a Glass Darkly: Vision of Integrated Community in Flannery

O'Connor's *Wise Blood*." *Contemporary Literature* 37.4 (1996): 559–85.

Eldred, Janet Carey. "Faulkner's Still Life: Art and Abortion in *The Wild Palms*." *Faulkner Journal* 4.1–2 (1988–89): 139–58.

Elie, Paul. *The Life You Save May Be Your Own: An American Pilgrimage*. New York: Farrar Straus Giroux, 2003.

Farmer, Joy A. "Mary Hood and the Speed of Grace: Catching Up with Flannery O'Connor." *Studies in Short Fiction* 33.1 (1996): 91–99.

Faulkner, William. "Address upon Receiving the Nobel Prize for Literature." *The Portable Faulkner*. Rev. ed. Ed. Malcolm Cowley. New York: Viking, 1967. 723–24.

———. "Delta Autumn." *The Portable Faulkner*. Rev. ed. Ed. Malcolm Cowley. New York: Viking, 1967. 635–61.

———. *Light in August. The Corrected Text*. New York: Vintage International, 1990.

———. *Novels 1936–1940*. New York: Library of America, 1990.

———. *Requiem for a Nun*. New York: Vintage, 1975.

———. *Selected Letters of William Faulkner*. Ed. Joseph Blotner. New York: Random House, 1978.

———. *Thinking of Home: William Faulkner's Letters to His Mother and Father, 1918–1925*. Ed. James G. Watson. New York: Norton, 1992.

Fitzgerald, F. Scott. *The Bodley Head Scott Fitzgerald*. Vol. I. London: Bodley Head, 1958.

———. *The Bodley Head Scott Fitzgerald*. Vol. 5 [Short Stories]. Selected and Introduced by Malcolm Cowley. London: Bodley Head, 1963.

Fitzgerald, F. Scott, and Zelda Fitzgerald. *Bits of Paradise: 21 Uncollected Stories by F. Scott and Zelda Fitzgerald*. Selected by Scottie Fitzgerald Smith and Matthew J. Bruccoli. London: Bodley Head, 1973.

Gammons, P. Keith. "The South of the Mind: The Changing Myth of the Lost Cause in the Life and Work of F. Scott Fitzgerald." *Southern Quarterly* 36.4 (1998): 106–12.

Giannone, Richard. *Flannery O'Connor: Hermit Novelist*. Urbana and Chicago: U of Illinois P, 2000.

Guroian, Vigen. *Tending the Heart of Virtue: How Classic Stories Awaken a Child's Moral Imagination*. New York: Oxford UP, 1998.

Havird, David. "The Saving Rape: Flannery O'Connor and Patriarchal Religion." *Mississippi Quarterly* 47.1 (1993): 15–27.

Holman, C. Hugh. "Fitzgerald's Changes on the Southern Belle: The Tarleton Trilogy." *The Short Stories of F. Scott Fitzgerald: New Approaches in Criticism*. Ed. Jackson R. Bryer. Madison: U of Wisconsin P, 1982. 53–64.

Hood, Mary. *Familiar Heat*. New York: Knopf, 1995.

Jeter, Ida. "*Jezebel* and the Emergence of the Hollywood Tradition of a Decadent South." *The South and Film*. Ed. Warren French. Jackson: UP of Mississippi, 1981. 31–46.

Johnson, Karen Ramsay. "Gender, Sexuality, and the Artist in Faulkner's Novels." *American Literature* 61.1 (1989): 1–16.

Josipovici, Gabriel. *On Trust: Art and the Temptations of Suspicion*. New Haven and London: Yale UP, 1999.

Kapur, Akash. "A Million Neuroses." <http://www.akashkapur.com/AkashKapurVSNaipaul/htm>.

Kimball, Roger. "Becoming Elias Canetti." *The New Criterion* 5.1 (1986): 17–28.

Kolakowski, Leszek. *The Presence of Myth*. Trans. Adam Czerniawski. Chicago: U of Chicago P, 1989.

———. "The Revenge of the Sacred in Secular Culture." *Modernity on Endless Trial*. Chicago: U of Chicago P, 1990. 63–74.

Kuehl, John. "Psychic Geography in 'The Ice Palace.'" *The Short Stories of F. Scott Fitzgerald: New Approaches in Criticism.* Ed. Jackson R. Bryer. Madison: U of Wisconsin P, 1982. 169–79.

Le Bon, Gustave. *The Crowd: A Study of the Popular Mind.* 4th Impression. London: T. Fisher Unwin, 1903.

Lowe, James. *The Creative Process of James Agee.* Baton Rouge: Louisiana State UP, 1994.

MacIntyre, Alasdair. *Whose Justice? Which Rationality?* South Bend: U of Notre Dame P, 1988.

Maritain, Jacques. "The End of Machiavellianism." In *Social and Political Philosophy.* 292–325.

———. "The Individual and the Person." In *Social and Political Philosophy.* 3–9.

———. *The Person and the Common Good.* New York: Charles Scribner's Sons, 1947.

———. *The Responsibility of the Artist.* New York: Scribner's, 1960.

———. "The Roots of Soviet Atheism." In *Social and Political Philosophy.* 252–63.

———. *The Social and Political Philosophy of Jacques Maritain: Selected Readings.* Ed. Joseph W. Evans and Leo R. Ward. New York: Charles Scribner's Sons, 1955.

Meyers, Jeffrey. "V. S. Naipaul and Paul Theroux." *PN Review* 26.3 (1999): 37–47.

Naipaul, V. S. "The Documentary Heresy." *Critical Perspectives on V. S. Naipaul.* Ed. Robert D. Hamner. Washington, D. C.: Three Continents Press, 1977. 23–25.

———. *The Enigma of Arrival.* New York: Vintage, 1988.

———. "Nobel Prize Lecture." http://www.nobel.se/literature/laureates/2001/naipaul-lecture-e.html>.

———. "Words are valuable." Interview with Tarun Tejpal. <http://www.tehelka.com/channels/literary/2001/oct/11/printable/lr101101finalpr/htm>.

O'Connor, Flannery. *Collected Works.* Ed. Sally Fitzgerald. New York: Library of America, 1988.

———. *The Habit of Being.* Ed. Sally Fitzgerald. 1979. New York: Noonday Press, 1988.

Porton, Richard. "The Politics of American Cinephilia: From the Popular Front to the Age of Video." *Cineaste* 27.4 (2002): 4–12.

Prigozy, Ruth. "Fitzgerald's Short Stories and the Depression: An Artistic Crisis." *The Short Stories of F. Scott Fitzgerald: New Approaches in Criticism.*" Ed. Jackson R. Bryer. Madison: U of Wisconsin P, 1982. 111–26.

Singal, Daniel J. *William Faulkner: The Making of a Modernist.* Chapel Hill: U of North Carolina P, 1997.

Spiegel, Alan. *James Agee and the Legend of Himself: A Critical Study.* Columbia: U of Missouri P, 1998.

Telotte, J. P. "The Human Landscape of John Ford's South." *The South and Film.* Ed. Warren French. Jackson: UP of Mississippi, 1981. 117–33.

Urgo, Joseph R. "Faulkner Unplugged: Abortopoesis and *The Wild Palms.*" *Faulkner and Gender.* Ed. Donald M. Kartiganer and Ann J. Abadie. Jackson: UP of Mississippi, 1996. 252–72.

Volpe, Edmond L. *A Reader's Guide to William Faulkner.* London: Thames and Hudson, 1966.

Weigel, George. "Mourning and Remembrance." *Wall Street Journal* 4 April 2005: A14.

Whitt, Margaret Earley. *Understanding Flannery O'Connor.* Columbia: U of South Carolina P, 1995.

Index

"Address upon Receiving the Nobel Prize for Literature" (Faulkner), 11, 13, 91, 129
Agee, James, 8–9, 69–84, 85; anarchism in, 76, 79–80; communism in, 79; fascism in, 81; free will in, 82; Holocaust in, 71, 81; libertarianism in, 79; materialism in, 70–71; skepticism in, 81; Works: *A Death in the Family*, 70–71, 74–75, 85; "Dream Sequence," 83; *Let Us Now Praise Famous Men* (with Walker Evans), 71–78, 83
Aiken, David, 113
anarchism, 9, 11, 13, 23, 47, 50, 76, 79–80, 105, 118, 125, 130
Arendt, Hannah, 5, 9, 13–14, 37, 54, 74–76, 78, 82
Aristotle, 6, 74
Armour, Robert A., 67 n 1

Bacon, Jon Lance, 97
Baldwin, James, 95–96
Barson, Alfred T., 74
Bellow, Saul, 129
Bergreen, Laurence 69, 71, 80–81, 83
Brooks, Cleanth, 32, 34–35

Calvinism, 18, 21, 25
Canetti, Elias, 5, 9, 11–26, 82; anarchism in, 13, 23; fascism in, 12; Holocaust in, 12; perfectibility of human nature in, 13; Stalinism in, 12; totalitarianism in, 6, 12–14; Work: *Crowds and Power*, 13–26, 82

Cash, Jean W., 85, 89–90, 98
Cold War, 97
communism, 79, 97–98
Crowds and Power (Canetti), 13–26, 82
culture of suspicion, 1, 3, 9

"Dance, The" (Fitzgerald), 64–65
Death in the Family, A (Agee), 70–71, 74–75, 85
"Delta Autumn" (Faulkner), 24
Desmond, John, 87
Dewey, John, 3
Dickens, Charles, 74–75
Dobbs, Cynthia, 32–34
"Dream Sequence" (Agee), 83
Dreiser, Theodore, 69–70

Edmunds, Susan, 86–88, 91–92
Eldred, Janet Carey, 32
Elie, Paul, 4
Enigma of Arrival, The (Naipaul), 119–30
Ethics (Aristotle), 74

Familiar Heat (Hood), 105–18
Farmer, Joy A., 108–09
fascism, 12, 24, 28, 81
Faulkner, William, 7, 10, 11–25, 27–42, 43–56, 91, 129–30; anarchism in, 11, 47, 50; Calvinism in, 18, 21, 25; fascism in, 12, 24, 28; free will in, 16; frontier in, 46–50; Holocaust in, 12; materialism in, 29; nihilism in, 28, 41, 50; perfectibility of human nature in, 29; racism in, 21–22; scapegoat figure in, 21–21; skepticism in, 11,

20, 50–51; Stalinism in, 12; states' rights in, 45; totalitarianism in, 6, 12–14, 28; Works: "Address upon Receiving the Nobel Prize for Literature," 11, 13, 91, 129; "Delta Autumn," 24; *If I Forget Thee, Jerusalem*, 27–42; *Light in August*, 15–20, 23; *Requiem for a Nun*, 43–56
"Fiction Writer and His Country, The" (O'Connor), 93
Fitzgerald, F. Scott, 7, 8, 57–68; materialism in, 57, 67; southern belle in, 57, 61–63, 65–67, 68 n 3; Works: "The Dance," 64–65; *The Great Gatsby*, 62, 65; "The Ice Palace," 62; "The Jelly-Bean," 60, 62; "The Last of the Belles," 57, 62–64; "The Popular Girl," 61; "The Swimmers," 60
Fitzgerald, Sally, 89, 103
Fitzgerald, Zelda Sayre, 61–64, 67, 68 n 5
Flye, Father, 74, 79–81
free will, 5, 16, 82, 98, 125
frontier, 46–50

Gammons, P. Keith, 61–63
Giannone, Richard, 93, 98, 100, 102–03
"Good Country People" (O'Connor), 89
Great Gatsby, The (Fitzgerald), 62, 65
Griffith, D. W., 67 n 1
Guroian, Vigen, 31

Habit of Being, The (O'Connor), 85, 90, 93, 95–96, 98, 104
Havird, David, 88–89
Hester, Betty, 87, 89–90, 96
Holocaust, 5, 12, 71, 81, 93
Hood, Mary, 8, 105–18; anarchism in, 105, 118; libertarianism in, 115, 117; relativism in, 105; skepticism in, 105; Work: *Familiar Heat*, 105–18
Human Condition, The (Arendt), 74

"Ice Palace, The" (Fitzgerald), 62
If I Forget Thee, Jerusalem (Faulkner), 27–42

"Jelly-Bean, The" (Fitzgerald), 60, 62
John Paul II, 1

Johnson, Karen Ramsay, 37
Josipovici, Gabriel, 1, 4, 98
Joyce, James, 122

Kafka, Franz, 77
Kapur, Akash, 129
King, Martin Luther, 96
Kirk, Russell, 104
Kolakowski, Leszek, 51, 113

"Last of the Belles, The" (Fitzgerald), 57, 62–64
Le Bon, Gustave, 25–26 n 1
Let Us Now Praise Famous Men (Agee with Walker Evans), 71–78, 83
libertarianism, 9, 79, 115, 117
Light in August (Faulkner), 15–20, 23
Little Dorrit (Dickens), 75
Lowe, James, 73, 75

Machiavelli, 90–91
MacIntyre, Alasdair, 5, 33–34
Marinetti, Emilio, 28–29
Maritain, Jacques, 46, 70–71, 86, 90–91, 97–98, 102, 104
materialism, 29, 57, 67, 70–71, 85, 89, 91, 97
McCarthy, Mary, 98, 104
Meyers, Jeffrey, 122

Naipaul, V. S., 7, 10, 119–30; anarchism in, 125, 130; free will in, 125; relativism in, 130; skepticism in, 122, 130; Works: *The Enigma of Arrival*, 119–30; "Nobel Prize Lecture," 119–120, 122
nihilism, 3, 5, 9, 28, 41, 50, 93
"Nobel Prize Lecture" (Naipaul), 119–120, 122

O'Connor, Flannery, 8, 85–104, 130; Cold War in, 97; communism in, 97–98; free will in, 98; Holocaust in, 93; materialism in, 85, 89, 91, 97; nihilism in, 93; relativism in, 98; Yadoo artists' colony in, 103; Works: "The Fiction Writer and His Country," 93; "Good Country People," 89; *The*

Habit of Being, 85, 90, 93, 95–96, 98, 104; *Wise Blood,* 86–87, 91–104

perfectibility of human nature, 1, 6, 13, 29
perspectivism, 5
Piaget, Jean, 3
"Popular Girl, The" (Fitzgerald), 61
Porton, Richard, 79
Prigozy, Ruth, 60

racism, 21–22
rationalism, 7
relativism, 2, 5–6, 9, 98, 105, 130
Requiem for a Nun (Faulkner), 43–56
Responsibility of the Artist, The (Maritain), 70
"Revenge of the Sacred" (Kolakowski), 113
Rogers, Will, 67–68 n 1

Saturday Evening Post, The, 58–60, 68 n 2
scapegoat figure, 20–21
Schreber, Daniel Paul, 22
Singal, Daniel J., 28, 30
skepticism, 1–3, 5–6, 9, 11, 20, 50–51, 81, 105, 122, 130
Smedley, Agnes, 103
southern belle, 57, 61–63, 65–67, 68 n 3
Spiegel, Alan, 73, 77–78
Spivey, Ted, 98
Stalinism, 12
states' rights, 45
"Swimmers, The" (Fitzgerald), 60

Tejpal, Tarun, 130
Telotte, J.P., 67 n 1
Time, 81
totalitarianism, 6, 12–14, 28

Urgo, Joseph, 38, 41

Volpe, Edmond, 30–31, 42

Weigel, George, 1
While You Were Sleeping, 114
Whitt, Margaret Earley, 100–01
Wise Blood (O'Connor), 86–87, 91–104
World War II, 12, 44, 71, 81, 93

Yadoo artists' colony, 103